SCENARIO PLANNING FOR LIBRARIES

JOAN GIESECKE
Editor

For the
Library and Information Technology Association
 and the
Library Administration and Management Association

American Library Association
Chicago and London   1998

The idea for this work grew out of material originally presented at a conference entitled "Transforming Libraries: A National Conference and Exhibition on Leadership and Technology in the Information Age," October 12–16, 1996, in Pittsburgh, Pennsylvania, sponsored by the Library Information Technology Association and the Library Administration and Management Association.

Project manager: Joan A. Grygel

Cover design: Richmond Jones

Text design: Dianne M. Rooney

Composition: the dotted i in Sabon and Perpetua using QuarkXpress v. 3.32

Printed on 50-pound Victor Offset, a pH-neutral stock, and bound in 10-point cover stock by Victor Graphics

The paper used in this publication meets the minimum requirements of American National Standard for Information Sciences—Permanence of Paper for Printed Library Materials, ANSI Z39.48-1992. ∞

Library of Congress Cataloging-in-Publication Data

Scenario planning for libraries / Joan Giesecke, editor.
    p.   cm.
  "For the Library and Information Technology Association and the Library Administration and Management Association."
  Papers originally presented at a conference entitled Transforming Libraries: a National Conference and Exhibition on Leadership and Technology in the Information Age, Oct. 12–16, 1996, in Pittsburgh, Pa.
  Includes bibliographical references and index.
  ISBN 0-8389-3482-X (alk. paper)
  1. Library planning—United States—Congresses. I. Giesecke, Joan. II. Library and Information Technology Association (U.S.). III. Library Administration and Management Association. IV. Transforming Libraries: a National Conference and Exhibition on Leadership and Technology in the Information Age (1996 : Pittsburgh, Pa.)
Z678.S35   1998
025.1—dc21   98-11027

Copyright © 1998 by the American Library Association. All rights reserved except those which may be granted by Sections 107 and 108 of the Copyright Revision Act of 1976.

Printed in the United States of America.

02   01   00   99   98   5   4   3   2   1

Contents

Figures *v*

Introduction *vii*

PART ONE
The Theory

1 Scenario Planning: Power Tools for Thinking about Alternatives   3
   JAMES KING

2 Radar vs. Road Map: Developing Strategies through Scenario Planning in an Uncertain World   18
   SCOT HORNICK AND JOAN GIESECKE

3 The Story: Tips on Writing Scenario Plots   26
   JOAN GIESECKE

4 Scenario Planning in the Learning Organization   34
   JOAN GIESECKE

Part Two
The Application

5 Arlington County Public Libraries Look to the Future   47
   CATHY ROBINSON, ANDY CINCOTTA, ROGER QUALTERS, AND ANN FRIEDMAN

6 Student Technology Fee: A Case Study at the University of Nebraska–Lincoln   79
   JIM EMAL AND JOAN GIESECKE

7 Preparing Librarians for the Twenty-First Century: Scenarios for the Future   95
   NANCY BUSCH

Suggested Readings   115

WWW Sites of Interest   119

Index   121

Figures

1.1 Futuring Matrix   4
2.1 Four Possible Scenarios for a Pharmaceutical Company   21
2.2 Managing the Portfolio of Strategic Options   25
5.1 Arlington County Public Libraries Factor Ranking   53
5.2 Arlington County Public Libraries Matrix of Most-Important Elements   56
5.3 Arlington County Public Libraries Scenario Matrix   58
6.1 UNL Matrix of Uses of Technology to Enhance Student Learning   83
6.2 UNL Student Technology Fee Scenario Matrix   86
6.3 Possible Uses for the UNL Technology Fee   87
7.1 Public Library Scenario Matrix   102
7.2 Scenario Matrix for Libraries of the Future   105

Introduction

Today's library managers face the very real dilemma of trying to steer their organizations through an uncertain, changing environment while agreeing to follow some sort of action plan. Governing boards, university administrators, state agencies, and citizen groups expect to find vision statements, goals and objectives, strategic plans, and action items laid out for the library system. But how can today's organization develop meaningful and useful plans when the environment is uncertain, technology constantly changes, and the competition for resources becomes more vicious?

Managers have tried any number of the latest management fads to address the problem of planning in an age of uncertainty. Their choices for techniques are numerous: strategic planning, long-range planning, short-range planning, crisis management, reengineering, redesigning, and reframing. In addition they have tried the quality initiative efforts, from total quality management to continuous-improvement initiatives. Any of these techniques can work. Just as easily, any of these techniques can result in nothing more than a large report or plan that takes up shelf space but has little relationship to the actual work and efforts of the organization. Successful managers take the parts of the various management techniques that work in their environment and ignore the rigid formalistic approach advocated in management texts.

Scenario driven planning is one planning technique that lends itself to today's uncertain environment and offers managers a flexible approach to viewing the future. In scenario driven planning, managers develop scenarios or stories to design possible futures. Using these stories, managers can then design strategies that will help move the organization forward. Scenario driven planning helps managers identify their assumptions about the future and the organization, describe their own mental models of the future, and then use that information to review and renew the organization.

The classic scenario driven planning experience is that of Royal Dutch Shell Corporation.[1] In the 1970s, Pierce Wack's corporate planning team was looking for events that might have an impact on the price of oil. Although the price of oil had been fairly steady for more than twenty years, the planning team realized that the situation could change. They looked for reasons why the Arabs would change the price of oil and developed two scenarios for the company: one where the price of oil remained steady and one where the price of oil rose sharply, creating an oil crisis. The team presented their data and waited for managers to react. Nothing happened. Wack and his team then developed new types of scenarios, ones that not only identified trends but also included the ramifications of possible changes in the environment. These stories helped managers imagine a very different future and allowed managers to look at how they could cope with and react to major changes in their environment. As a consequence of this new approach to scenario development, the managers at Royal Dutch Shell were able to respond quickly when the unthinkable happened: the 1973 oil crisis.

The result of the scenario planning exercise was not an accurate description of the future. Instead the exercise was an opportunity for managers to design strategies to help the organization create its own future as the environment changed. Managers could make better decisions because they had discussed and imagined a *variety* of plausible futures rather than planning for one possible future.

Scenario driven planning is not only a technique that can be used for a major strategic planning effort; it also works for addressing narrower strategic issues. Part 1 of this book describes the basic technique for developing and using scenarios in the planning process. In chapter 1, James King describes the eight steps that provide a basic outline for the process of developing scenarios. These flexible steps allow organizations to adapt to a continuously changing environment. Scot Hornick uses the differences between sophisticated navigational technology and old-fashioned road maps as an analogy to compare and contrast traditional strategy formulation with scenario planning in chapter 2. Chapter 3 provides helpful tips on writing scenario plots. Joan Giesecke describes the challenges of developing story lines or plots that are meaningful and carefully addresses issues raised in the planning process. The chapter describes the limiting nature of information filters and provides in-depth discussion of three major plot lines. Chapter 4 wraps up part I with a description of how scenario planning can be used as a technique to assist organizations in becoming learning organizations. Joan Giesecke, author of chapters 3 and 4, has experience with both learning organizations and scenario planning.

Part 2 includes three case studies showing how organizations have used scenario planning. The first case is that of a public library system's use of the technique to redesign the system's strategic plan in Arlington County, Virginia, Public Libraries. Included in the chapter is information on forming a scenario planning team, training necessary to function as a team, and the environment necessary for a scenario planning process to work. Also included is a detailed section on how to develop scenarios and the necessity of vision and mission to the process. Of particular interest to readers interested in trying scenario driven planning is the section on hindsight and lessons learned.

The next case shows how scenario planning can be used to address a strategic issue. The authors describe how the techniques helped them implement a student technology fee at a large research university. They describe the makeup of the planning group, the process of devising scenarios, and the benefits of using scenario planning for long-range possibilities as well as short-term needs. Two final scenarios from the planning process are included.

Finally, the third case study shows how scenarios can be used to advance a statewide discussion on the broad issue of the role of library professionals in the twenty-first century. Author Nancy Busch describes four possible scenarios for the future of Nebraska's public library and information professionals. The driving force behind the need to develop the scenarios is the question of what critical skills are going to be necessary for the twenty-first century. This question is timely and pertinent for all libraries and librarians. Its content can easily be applied by librarians and information professionals working in other states.

The idea for the book came from the LAMA/LITA National Conference program on scenario planning. I wish to thank the conference publication committee and the program participants for their work in helping to create this book.

Note

1. For a complete description of the Shell Oil case, see Peter Schwartz, *The Art of the Long View: Planning for the Future in an Uncertain World* (New York, N.Y.: Currency Books, 1991), 7–10.

Part One

The Theory

1

Scenario Planning
Powerful Tools for Thinking about Alternatives

JAMES KING
ASSOCIATE PROFESSOR
UNIVERSITY OF NEBRASKA–LINCOLN

By definition, the future is unknown. This means that there are many possibilities of what could be. All individuals and organizations have countless options for the future. The working assumption is that multiple "futures" exist out there.

Given the idea of several possible futures, people and organizations can, do, and should create their own futures. These days, we do not accept the fatalistic idea of just letting things happen to us. We can create futures by considering alternatives to the present—where we are now and how we are acting now. Then we build our futures by examining options for accepted activities and considering new strategies for implementation. Finally, we construct futures from the abundant possibilities of what might be. We set up specific actions to take advantage of the opportunities we have seen in our future, avoiding the problems we anticipate.

Today does not just happen. We design today to achieve and make our ideal futures happen.

With the future many unknowns persist. How can we explore and study "a" future? What are strategies to study the future?

Futurists have many ways of exploring this interesting area. One useful conceptual tool, shown in figure 1.1, is a matrix originally developed by Bishop and King. This matrix highlights three approaches to understanding futures thinking: probable, possible, and preferable futures.[1] While these futures are discussed separately, people frequently combine them. Many tools and techniques are used simultaneously to give planners a rich and robust peek at a future.

Probable Futures

Probable futures are the most familiar. Key trends and the constraints of current situations are the critical elements driving probable futures. This type of futures thinking uses definite, analytical, rational ways of considering what will happen and what is probable. To study and design probable futures, we extrapolate from the present to the future, examine demographic trends, and develop implications for continuation, increases, or declines in many services. Analogies and history also help determine and explain what may or will probably happen next. For example, in some public institutions, the end of the fiscal year brings the release of "saved" or "recov-

Figure 1.1 Futuring Matrix

Types of Futures	Driving Forces	Types of Thinking	Techniques to Study/Design
Probable	Constants Trends	Definite Scientific	Historical analogy Extrapolation
Possible	Discontinuities Surprises	Speculative Imaginative	Scenario development Delphi
Preferable	Choices Images	Visionary Empowered	Visioning Strategic planning

Source: From P. Bishop and J. W. King, "Vision-Driven Change in Higher Education: A National Visioning Project" (paper presented at the World Future Society Meeting, Washington, D.C., 17 July 1996).

ered" monies that may be used for equipment. This history of released money may be somewhat constant on a yearly basis. As a result, many decision makers may even develop expenditure planning based on this money, an expected probable future based on the past.

Possible Futures

A different group of futures resides in the "possible." In possible futures, we are looking for surprises. We scan beyond and behind trends to discover the discontinuities of today's events. What is changing that we cannot see? What might be changing if we could see better or had a different view? What would we envision if we had better, more, or other data? Imagination and speculative thinking are the powerful conceptual tools associated with this approach. Scenario development is one well-publicized technique for thinking about possible futures.

Preferable Futures

In preferable futures individuals or organizations develop images or visions of what they prefer. They discuss idealized states or conditions. The processes of preferable futures are often full of energy and result in excellent direction and guidelines for action. Nevertheless, the process has to move beyond discussion of change. Using the vision they develop, groups then convert it into specific action agendas through techniques such as strategic planning. People are often "empowered" during the group processes as they help imagine and choose preferable futures.

Scenarios: Exploring and Thinking about the Future

The focus of the rest of this chapter will be on scenario development, a practical and dynamic tool to envision possible futures. The process of scenario building generates abundant fresh ideas about issues of concern or key decisions to be made. By using scenarios, people can generate novel and innovative approaches to solving problems.

When developing scenarios, people frequently find they have given themselves fertile alternatives and powerful options for action. By using scenarios, groups can anticipate change and think "out of the box." This mental stretching may result in devising solutions to stumbling blocks that do not yet exist or are not yet seen in their institution. They may develop strategies to avoid problems or, perhaps, find exciting and rare opportunities for growth and development in emerging issues.

Scenarios can be viewed as organizational learning.[2] When groups develop scenarios and when results are shared widely, many people can learn and profit from the experiences. They may, in fact, develop new mental models "about what has been and what might be."[3] In turn, this helps the organization grow and learn. Organizational learning and scenario planning are explored further in chapter 4.

What Are Scenarios?

In working with scenarios, Schwartz and Wack warn against getting too detailed in defining both words and processes.[4] With scenarios, we are discussing things that might be. Exactness is not prized. While this "fuzziness" of scenario development may be a problem to concrete thinkers, they can quickly grasp the stories and narratives that emerge from the scenario development process. Their analytic skills will provide insights into the underlying assumptions and possible implications. Abstract and intuitive thinkers may wander too far from the themes and logic of the scenarios. In the end, this group will add lots of "what ifs" in discovering implications. From this rich, fuzzy mix of people and processes, better decision making will result.

Scenarios can be an integral part of the planning process. Van der Heijden notes that one group saw scenario development "as a way to plan without having to predict things that everyone knew were unpredictable."[5] As a broad guideline, Schwartz describes the scenario as

> a tool for ordering one's perceptions about alternative future environments in which one's decisions might be played out. Alter-

natively: a set of organized ways for us to dream effectively about our own future. Concretely, they resemble a set of stories, either written out or often spoken. However, these stories are built around carefully constructed "plots" that make the significant elements of the world scene stand out boldly.[6]

Simply, scenarios are stories about possible futures. These stories are speculative, imaginative, and responsive to questions about those futures. While based on today's information and trends, scenarios extrapolate from the present and consider future possibilities. Scenario development is not geared to predict or forecast the future; rather, it aims to discuss possibilities and to develop strategies for dealing with those possibilities. The scenario narratives are plausible futures, not science fiction or futuristic noveling.

Ogilvy describes what good scenarios should achieve:

> a narrative synthesis of many details into a story about the future that makes sense of the present. And there are always several such stories for any given present.[7]

There is no one best scenario. Usually there will be several (two to four) narratives for consideration.

For our use, consider several assumptions about scenarios. Scenarios are

- energy creating
- direction giving
- based on today's information and trends
- projections beyond tomorrow
- plausible
- based on assumptions that can be made visible

We can also say what scenarios are not. They are not

- predictions or forecasts
- totally fiction
- guidelines for action or specific strategic direction

Scenarios give us insights into possibilities. The future is still uncertain.

To benefit from scenarios, there must be a question or a specific focus of concern. Generally, the question will take a form such as the following:

What are the key decisions that will need to be made?

What are the key issues involved in the work/organization?

What are the themes or driving forces around the work/issue/organization?

The question helps structure the narrative. Rich and deep stories emerge from the scenarios when there is much information, in particular about social, technological, economic, environmental, and political issues (known by their acronym, STEEP). In the library and education field we would also highlight educational information. Thus, along with a good question, issue, or decision to start the process, we need good information. This leads us to look at how we can prepare scenarios.

Eight Steps for Developing Scenarios

There are many excellent scenario development processes. However, the general procedures used by Schwartz and discussed by Duncan and Wack; May; Senge and others; Schoemaker and van der Heijden; and Wack are easily adaptable by many groups. (See the Further Reading at the end of this book.)

While the scenario process is flexible, it is present as a series of interlinked steps. The following sections describe each step or phase in the process and present some options to the general, overall scenario development process. This is not a one-day process. Much time must be committed to make the scenario development process and all the steps fit together to provide a futures story.

STEP 1

Identify and choose the central point or decision to be made.

To start the scenario development process, practitioners have to identify the key concerns that will guide the actual thinking and writing. This process puts the issues out front for all to see in print.

Questions to help identify and choose the central point or decision include both narrow, specific questions and broad, global questions.

Why are we doing this?

What is the key decision on the horizon?

What are the long-term, complex decisions that we must make?

What is the predominant item we are trying to decide?

What is motivating us?

What have we previously dismissed?

The outcome of this diagnosis should be the identification of a vital issue to the organization or key decision to be made by the group. In turn, the issue or decision will structure and provide the framework for the development of the scenario.

Examples of a central point might be the following:

What will be the chief delivery mode for our services in the next ten years?

What is the future of enrollment here?

What type of administrative structure should we have to manage services in the twenty-first century?

How do we better satisfy our clients?

Sometimes, of course, key concerns arise from outside decisions or events and point to clear issues to be studied. For these situations, we know what the issues are; we know what the questions are. Regardless, this step is still necessary. New ways of viewing old issues may surface.

Often the issues or questions are fuzzy; team members do not agree on the core question. Methods to clarify the question include trigger interviews and group processes involving discussion and consensus.[8] Questions such as the following will guide the process:

What is the major decision we must make in the near future?

What are the long-term, complex decisions that we should make?

What is the primary element we are trying to decide?

A note of caution. For the scenario process to be successful, many players must be involved, including those who have a stake in the decision. Thus, consumers, managers, students, faculty, staff, and administration must be included. This broad audience will bring many viewpoints to the table and make for a robust discussion.

STEP 2
Identify the key forces in the environment.

Every work environment has major developments, forces, and trends molding and shaping it. This step asks: What are the developments or driving forces that might influence the issues specified in step 1? Team members will want to detect and identify key environmental forces and trends. Trends are changes in the direction of an event. Usually, these are long-term changes. Sometimes trends are increasing slowly or quickly; sometimes trends are declining. Others are growing or declining exponentially while some are moving in a direction, with quick jumps up or down. There can also be seasonal trends. Thus, in this step, we identify the central trends, events and forces that are causing the major issue noted in step 1.

Questions to help identify these trends include:

What things impress on the issue or decision in a major way?

What fundamental social, technological, environmental, economic, and political forces and trends can be identified that will influence the issue or decision?

What are the positive and negative forces that should be considered?

From this step will emerge a group of factors that can move the issue. These forces are now fashioning or could soon be shaping the future of the organization or group. To think of these forces, though, team members must be flexible. In *The Art of the Long View* Schwartz stresses that "flexibility of perspective is critical. You simultaneously focus on questions that matter to you and keep your awareness open for the unexpected."[9] Team members have to look at lots of information from extremely wide varieties of sources. Generally, a good place to start is with STEEP groupings—social, technological, economic, environmental, and political information, along with education as a category. Examples of factors that might be important are

- costs
- quality of programs
- increased competition for students
- competencies of new staff

Several processes specify forces in these categories. These include a variety of information-gathering and sharing methods plus group methods that generate lists, group discussion, use of experts, scanning processes, and common knowledge of the local environment. Note this last point: common knowledge often is not shared, and those close to events often miss key driving forces. Discussing what people know about local forces and trends shaping the event builds community and makes unusual things "common."

STEP 3

List and analyze those important driving forces.

To deal with the future, we need to notice and perceive key trends and events. We also need to understand how they might influence the issues under consideration.

Of these forces,

- Which are predictable and which are uncertain?
- What are the main trends?
- In what direction are they moving?
- How fast and with how much force are they changing?
- Over which ones may we still have some control and some choice?
- What is novel?
- What major trend breaks can be identified?
- What major trends will continue?

In the scenario development process, step 3 can be the most research-intensive.[10] Listing and analyzing the important driving forces will require examining many emerging trends and the driving pressures and assumptions behind them. Consider demographics, funding tendencies, new hires, innovative but not yet carried out ideas, and a host of other factors and forces. Within all this, there will be much uncertainty and vagueness.

Again, the STEEP categories (society—demographics, technology—electronic media, economics—costs, environment—actual/public perceptions, and politics—policies and regulations) are useful in organizing the trends and forces. What events are predetermined (like some demographics)? What is very uncertain (like student opinion)? What about perception? Sometimes perceived events and forces (not really actual) act as powerful agents and must be considered. The product of this step will be a description of the environment in which the decision must be made.

As a research step, methods such as scanning and strategic-trend intelligence provide a systemic approach. (See Suggested Readings.)

STEP 4

Rank the forces.

Next, rank or order the major forces by their importance to the key issue and their level of uncertainty.

Given these trends and forces, what is their importance to the chief issue?

Which are the more important forces given the decision?

Which trends are most basic for the success of the issue?

What is their level of uncertainty?

Which forces are known and which are puzzles?

Two or three factors or forces that are most important to the issue or decision and most uncertain will emerge from this step. These factors will be used to identify scenario themes.

Using a matrix to study the interaction of the forces and trends with the issue/decision is one approach to developing a ranking.[11] Nominal group processes and other ranking methods can also be used.

STEP 5

Choose the main themes or assumptions to develop the scenarios.

Step 5 is the selection of the scenario logics. From these themes, different scenarios will be built. Different themes will lead to different futures. Select those assumptions, themes, and logics that will be important to the group who will deal with the key issue or decision to be made. What are the most "powerful forces" driving the decision? What are the major trends colliding with the issue?

The themes chosen will not be good, bad, or average. Rather, the themes will grow out of the interplay of forces and trends. For example, in studying new educational environments, two key driving forces emerged: first the teachers' need for new technologies for both research and teaching, and second, the demand by students for more multimedia education. From these two themes, several scenarios could be developed. First, we could envision a story in which teachers had access to, but did not use, technology in teaching students hungry for multimedia education. We could write another narrative in which teachers did use technology and worked with students both to develop new instruction and to deliver old content via multimedia channels.

STEP 6

Complete or develop the scenarios.

Creating a narrative sequence of events that shows possible and plausible happenings is the next step. These narratives will be stories. Each scenario should "centre [sic] around the impact of each of the scenario themes on the driving forces identified earlier."[12]

While the scenario will contain enough detail to make it interesting and influential for the decision to be made, it also has to be easy to understand. No scenario can cover all events or consider all implications. That is why identifying the most compelling driving forces and assessing their influence and their uncertainty is so important.

In the end we want to have a few scenarios, usually two to four. We will develop stories "whose differences make a difference to decision makers."[13] Do not worry about how likely, or unlikely, the narratives may be. The focus continues to be on the scenario's ability to enlighten the issue or decision.[14]

Consider the previous issue: new educational environments. We identified key driving forces—the teachers' needs for new technologies for both research and teaching and the student demand for multimedia education. These two themes allow us to develop plots for our scenarios. The decision/key issue will determine how we actually write our scenario, but Schwartz notes that three plots appear regularly.[15] First is "winners and losers," where conflict occurs, compromise results, yet someone "loses."

A second plot is "challenge and response." In this plot, new and unexpected situations are faced repeatedly, and the organization or individual surfaces from each situation with some new responses—positive, negative, or neutral.

The final plot is "evolution." Scenarios with the evolution plot show slow change. This change can be either positive or negative, but it is often change to which we are not normally oriented.

Schwartz identifies several other plots: revolution—sudden and dramatic change; cycles—growth, development, decline, and regrowth; infinite possibility—expansion and improvement; Lone Ranger—individual against the system; my generation—the influence of culture on peoples' values.[16] These plots are explained in greater detail in chapter 3.

In developing scenarios, some plots will intermingle and interact through reflection and discussion until we have decided to go with a particular theme or plot. Nevertheless, several plots and subplots run through each scenario. The key will be developing a logical rationale to structure the writing of the scenario.

For example, in an evolutionary scenario, we can envision growth in a department driven by ballooning enrollment. It could also be confined by increasing budget cuts and lack of students. The entry of new faculty with new skills might rearrange a department. All these "logics" will structure the complete scenario.

The development of the scenarios can also be guided by criteria developed by Morrison and Wilson:

> They should be plausible, within the limits of what might happen.
> They should be "structurally different," not simply variations of a single case.

Each scenario should be internally consistent with events and trends leading to certain outcomes that have a logic.

They should have "decision-making utility," the ability to help us understand the issue and the decision.

The scenarios ought to challenge the conventional wisdom about the future of the organization.[17]

STEP 7
Look at the scenario implications.

The entire idea of developing scenarios is to make reasonable decisions in the face of uncertainty. To do this, we have to look at the implications of the scenarios we have just developed.

What are each scenario's impacts on the issues or decisions identified in step 1? Return to the focal issue and look at the decision in each scenario.

Are there common themes that emerge across all issues?

Are there certain decisions that will be generic in other conditions?

Do the scenarios suggest particular points or issues that should be monitored?

A scenario should clarify the choices to be made, or it should provide fresh and novel insights into the issues. What ideas and concerns are rising? What is falling? What are early signs of success or problems? A SWOT analysis (looking at strengths, weaknesses, opportunities, and threats) is also a useful method to study implications.

The discussion around scenario implications will help create a "learning community" in the organization. Common themes and values will appear. Strange and weird possibilities will emerge. People will enlarge their own perspectives and will develop inventive viewpoints.

STEP 8
Identify indicators that will help in monitoring changes as they develop.

Finally, what indicators will help the organization determine and monitor change? By examining the scenario implications, we now have an idea of what indicators to observe to help us monitor change. By choosing certain indicators to follow, we can peek into the future and gain insights. We can "know" in advance what may happen to influence certain of our management decisions.

After going through this scenario development process, monitoring real-world changes in selected indicators will suggest "orderly" implications for real-world actions.

What will be indicators of change?
What connections are there?
What influences what?
What may change over time?
In what directions should we be looking?

Scanning techniques used earlier are good methods to monitor change. All participants in the group can be responsible for monitoring the chief indicators while still being open to an array of other possible influences.

The Outcome

These eight steps provide a basic outline for developing scenarios. They can be adapted in many ways to increase their power for any group.

From choosing the central point or decision to monitoring indicators, we have developed a powerful process to think about plausible futures. The organization has engaged in studying itself in a systematic and enjoyable fashion. At times, there will be lots of discussion, lots of fuzzy issues, and lots of lack of consensus. The result of the scenario development process will be stronger organizations and competent individuals who know the current environment. While uncertainty will not be vanquished, we now have a community thinking about the future, and we will have excitement and direction for the future.

Notes

1. R. Amara, "Views on Futures Research Methodology," *Futures* 23 (July/Aug. 1991): 645–9.
2. A. P. de Geus, "Planning as Learning," *Harvard Business Review* 66, no. 2 (1988): 70–4.
3. P. M. Senge, *The Fifth Discipline* (New York: Currency Doubleday, 1990), 8–9.
4. P. Schwartz, *The Art of the Long View: Planning for the Future in an Uncertain World* (New York: Currency Doubleday, 1991); P. Wack, "Scenarios: Shooting the Rapids," *Harvard Business Review* 63, no. 6 (1985): 139–50.
5. K. van der Heijden, *Scenarios: The Art of Strategic Conversation* (New York: John Wiley, 1996), 16.
6. Schwartz, *The Art of the Long View*, 4.
7. P. Ogilvy, "Futures Studies and the Human Sciences: The Case for Normative Scenarios," in *New Thinking for a New Millennium*, ed. R. A. Slaughter (New York: Routledge, 1996), 42.
8. P. M. Senge and others, *The Fifth Discipline Fieldbook: Strategies and Tools for Building a Learning Organization* (New York: Currency Doubleday, 1994).
9. Schwartz, *The Art of the Long View*, 61.
10. Schwartz, *The Art of the Long View*, 61.
11. J. L. Morrison and I. Wilson, *Planning and Management for a Changing Environment: A Handbook on Redesigning Post Secondary Institutions* (San Francisco: Jossey-Bass, nd., forthcoming).
12. G. H. May, *The Future Is Ours: Foreseeing, Managing and Creating the Future* (Westport, Conn.: Praeger, 1996), 165.
13. Schwartz, *The Art of the Long View*, 243.
14. P. M. Senge and others, *The Fifth Discipline Fieldbook*, 276.
15. Schwartz, *The Art of the Long View*, 147.
16. Schwartz, *The Art of the Long View*, 157–64.
17. Morrison and Wilson, *Planning and Management for a Changing Environment*.

2

Radar vs. Road Map

Developing Strategies through Scenario Planning in an Uncertain World

SCOT HORNICK
ANDERSEN CONSULTING

JOAN GIESECKE
DEAN OF LIBRARIES
UNIVERSITY OF NEBRASKA–LINCOLN

Imagine you are cruising along at Mach 1.2 in an advanced fighter aircraft. You want to stay on course to reach your destination while traveling through a changing, uncertain environment. You need to be able to anticipate problems, avoid hazards, and quickly adjust your course as conditions change. Which would you rather have as a navigational tool: radar or a road map?

Traditional strategy formulation focuses on determining the right things to do and developing a road map to success. Managers can then concentrate on executing plans to achieve their goals based on that map. In most industries today, though, accelerating technology, fickle consumers, and nimble competitors render the road maps dated almost as fast as they can be printed, leaving managers to wonder how to deal with the shrinking "mean time between surprises."

Based on a presentation by Dr. Scot Hornick, Andersen Consulting, at the LAMA/LITA Conference, October 1996. Drafted with Joan Giesecke.

Both the increase in the frequency of changes and the increase in the unpredictability of these changes have led to a turbulent environment that is characterized by continuous surprises. Changes in the three key trend areas of technology, social structure of society, and government policy can leave managers wondering if planning is even possible or if crisis management is the only alternative left to them.

Operating in an environment of shrinking mean time between surprises creates a strategic uncertainty in which

- it is difficult to set a single direction when there are multiple possible future worlds
- linear extrapolations of trends are poor predictors of the discontinuities that seem to be the dominant themes in any future vision
- force-fitting the future into a tunnel vision may set you up to be blindsided

How can managers prepare for surprises in today's uncertain environment?

While the road map paradigm works well in a stable environment, companies today need to achieve an evolving set of objectives, track emerging threats and opportunities, and at the same time keep flying. Managers using a road map paradigm believe that

- ultimate objectives are known, perhaps because someone has achieved them before
- the terrain is stable
- detours are generally well marked
- the rules of the road do not change
- the world responds slowly to change

Managers who view the world from the paradigm of a fighter pilot believe that

- objectives are evolving and uncertain
- organizations must keep moving or they will crash
- threats and opportunities are constantly changing
- there is no fixed frame of reference
- there are no rules

The information field is now in an environment that resembles the fighter pilot rather than the road map paradigm. In such a changing environment, traditional strategic planning techniques are insufficient to ensure success. Instead managers must use different, more-dynamic techniques to examine possible futures and to plan for uncertainty. Scenario planning is one such technique.

The Structure of Scenarios

Scenarios are tools for helping organizations take a long view in a world of great uncertainty.[1] The scenario visioning process begins with an underlying question or decision and then develops alternate stories about the future. For each story, planners then develop a set of strategic implications.

Beyond this it is also important to explain what scenarios are not. They are not bounded by today's world and are not limited to excluding the unthinkable. They are not exact predictions of the future. They are not mutually exclusive of each other and they are not governed by the laws of probability. Scenarios are plausible futures, not a single prediction of the future.

Example of Scenario Visioning

An example of scenario visioning from the pharmaceutical industry illustrates this technique. A pharmaceutical company, using scenario planning techniques, began with the question, "What will be the role of our company in the health care value delivery model in the year 2002?" After identifying about thirty-five to forty-five driving forces in their field, they isolated the two independent factors that seemed to be the most important and the most uncertain: the value of pharmaceutical and medical product innovation and the power of the physicians/patients vs. that of the care management companies and insurers. As shown in figure 2.1, these two factors form the axis of a matrix outlining four possible scenarios for the company. Each scenario yields different strategies for the pharmaceutical firms:

Figure 2.1 Four Possible Scenarios for a Pharmaceutical Company

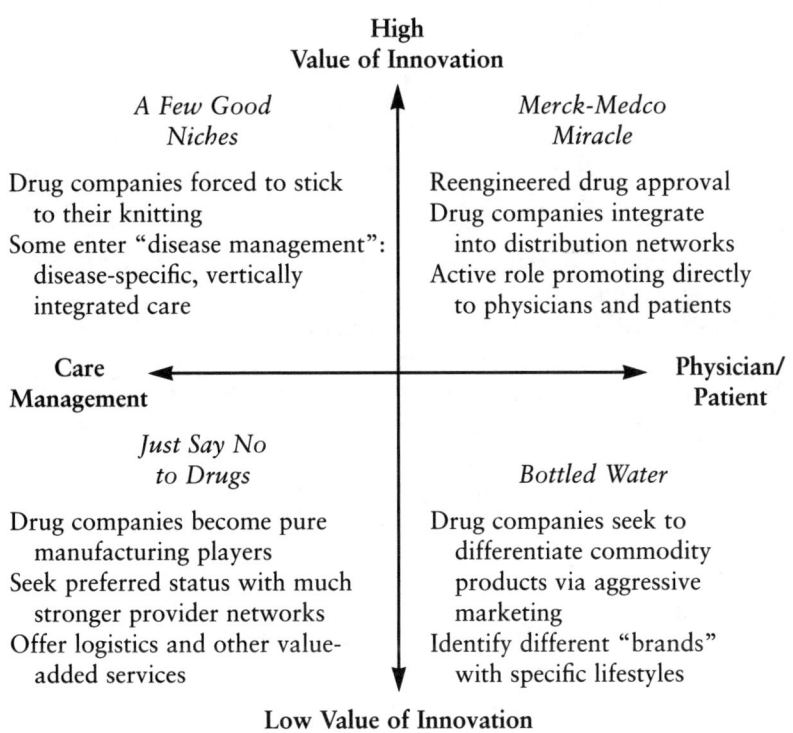

Source: Scot Hornick, Andersen Consulting

A Few Good Niches. If innovation is valued in the future and if the health care industry is dominated by care management companies, a pharmaceutical company is likely to concentrate on a few key drugs and become known for treating certain diseases. The drug company becomes a partner in the vertical integration of care providers for patients with that disease.

Merck-Medco Miracle. If innovation is valued and physicians retain control of patient care, then drug companies could continue strategies to promote their products directly to physicians and patients in an effort to have an active role in the decision making about the disease-treatment system.

Just Say No to Drugs. If innovation is not valued and care management companies dominate the health care arena, then drug companies might become pure manufacturing firms and seek preferred provider status with major care conglomerates.

Bottled Water. If innovation is not valued and physicians control health care decisions, then drug companies could try to differentiate products through aggressive marketing and brand name identification.

Once the basic outline of the stories is developed, planners write more-detailed narratives to highlight issues and likely outcomes that will have an impact on the organization if the scenario proves to be a realistic prediction of the future. Included in the description process is the creation of a comprehensive list of early warning signs to alert the organization that events are moving toward the proposed scenario and that action is warranted to respond to the changes. Scenario writing also includes the listing of specific implications for the organization for the given scenario.

Types of Strategies

The power of scenario visioning comes from consideration of the implications of the scenarios for the organization, that is, "How will we have to change to be successful in these possible new worlds?" The strategies can be classified according to the breadth of their applicability: robust, contingent, and losing strategies.

Robust strategies are are of two types. First, there are strategies that hold under all scenarios. These can be classified as "no-brainers." Second are those strategies that hold well under some scenarios and are essentially indifferent in others. These can be classified as "no painers."

Contingent implications are those that hold well under some scenarios but may be adverse under others. These strategies can yield "big gains/big pains."

Losing propositions are those initiatives that are ill-advised under all scenarios.

Choosing Strategies

Organizations should examine the implications and strategies developed under each scenario and choose those that are most likely to succeed or do the least amount of damage if they fail.

Strategies focused on the most probable scenario or directed toward a specific future ignore the value scenarios provide. Development of fixed strategies from multiple scenarios can limit an organization to working with the equivalent of a static road map. Even multiple fixed strategies can have the same end result.

On the other hand, most organizations do not have the resources to pursue each discrete future separately. Rather than concentrate on fixed strategies, organizations need to think in terms of emergent strategies or the development, refinement, and alteration of strategies as the conditions of the organization change. As managers begin to examine the scenarios they have developed, they are most likely to concentrate on robust strategies: those strategies that are effective across almost all scenarios. Although these strategies may initially limit options for the organization, the strategies do provide the organization with a path to follow to begin creating the organization's own futures. As time goes on and conditions change, the scenarios become more distinctive, and there is less overlap among the plausible futures. Organizations can then modify and change strategies and begin to incorporate contingent strategies as well as robust strategies into their plans.

However, in some situations, the opportunity to exploit contingent implications may be lost if specific actions are not taken to ensure that the opportunity will exist in the future. Under these circumstances, it may be wise to purchase an option on these strategies. Much like its counterpart in the financial world, an option is an action or investment that provides decision makers with the opportunity—but not the obligation—to take advantage of future events that would not be possible without the earlier activities or investment. Substantial value can be created by designing and managing options to expand or modify initiatives as conditions warrant, to defer the activity or investment until conditions improve, or to terminate the activity or investment if conditions become unfavorable.

In choosing strategies for implementation, an organization begins with robust strategies and purchases options on contingent strategies. (See figure 2.2.) As time passes and the scenarios become more distinctive, organizations evaluate and select new alternatives. It is now time for an organization to exercise flexible options as it manages its options portfolio. Flexible options are those options that allow the organization to implement strategies that fall between robust and contingent strategies. These strategies may result in some pain to the organization but are more likely to bring gains to the organization.

As the differences between scenarios and reality become more extreme, the organization is better able to choose among the scenarios and the strategies associated with each scenario. With the further passage of time the organization again evaluates the risks of implementing contingent strategies. The organization exercises options on contingent strategies when the risk of implementing the strategy is at an acceptable level for the organization. This process of managing a portfolio of strategic options provides organizations with flexibility that is needed to respond to and thrive in an uncertain, chaotic environment.

Scenario planning provides managers with a set of tools to help them develop a portfolio of strategic options so that organizations can adjust to change, minimize the crises, and anticipate surprises that are characteristic of an uncertain future. In other words, scenario planning provides managers with the radar they need to navigate in uncertain times and helps them to not become locked into a road map mentality.

Note

1. P. Schwartz, *The Art of the Long View: Planning for the Future in an Uncertain World* (New York: Currency Doubleday, 1991), 4.

Figure 2.2 Managing the Portfolio of Strategic Options

Time Frame: Today ⟶ Future

Evaluating Scenarios	Undifferentiated scenarios	Limited differentiation of scenarios	Moderate to extreme differentiation of scenarios
Organizational Choices	Act on robust strategies Purchase options	Exercise flexible options Evaluate and select new alternatives Manage option portfolio	Exercise contingent options Evaluate and select new alternatives Manage option portfolio

Source: Scot Hornick, Andersen Consulting

3

The Story
Tips on Writing Scenario Plots

JOAN GIESECKE
DEAN OF LIBRARIES
UNIVERSITY OF NEBRASKA–LINCOLN

Storytelling is an effective way of conveying information about an organization. Stories help staff members understand the past and describe the present. They outline organizational values, hopes, and visions. "Tell the company's story" is a standard piece of management advice to relay ideas and help staff relate to and accept the organizational view of the environment.

In scenario planning, the story or plot line is the foundation for the planning process. Composing a plot or story that is meaningful while addressing the key issues raised in the planning process is the challenge for scenario planning participants. Like a good short story or screen play, the story must have a logical structure that the audience can follow, be believable to the audience, and capture the audience's imagination. If a plot is too far afield, it will be dismissed as unattainable and useless. If the plot is too mundane, managers will not be challenged to consider strategic alternatives. If the plot is boring and tedious, it will be ignored. If it is too fanciful, it will be dismissed as fiction. For scenario writing to be successful, then, the story must be believable, the audience must be able to relate to the elements of the plot, and the story must address the key issues of concern to the audience.

Framing the Problem

The first step in the scenario process is to frame the problem in a way that captures the imaginations of the participants. In an uncertain environment, identifying the central points of the problem and framing the issues is as important as developing solutions. Technologies to aid managers in problem framing are included in strategic planning methodologies. One technique that may be particularly useful in scenario planning and that can aid in plot development is that of strategic assumption surfacing and testing (SAST).[1] In this technique, participants work backward from strategies to data to identifying the underlying assumptions that frame how they solve the problem. Participants then have the opportunity to discuss and review their assumptions about the problem. They can identify and drop assumptions that are implausible or counterproductive and develop a list of assumptions that frame how they wish to view the problem at hand. Uncovering the hidden assumptions in the planning process helps managers reorganize the mental models they use to make decisions. The assumptions, then, become the framework for designing a plot or story.

Writing for Change

Once managers have identified the underlying assumptions that frame how they view the problem, they can begin to develop alternative strategies or approaches to address the problem.

To successfully design changes in strategies, participants should identify and consider the potential for resistance to proposed changes and possible attitudes by staff about the changes that can result in a failure to implement change.[2] To address possible resistance to change, plot writers need to consider internal inertia that prevents change as well as external conditions that may limit control of the environment. How participants respond to external change or threats depends in part on how they view the organization. Viewing the organization as a fixed entity is likely to result in strategies that are basically incremental responses to the environment. Although this view may be quite effective in a fairly stable environment, in an uncertain environment participants may be more effective if they view the organization as fluid. One metaphor of organizations that can help participants is to view the organization as a mobile tent, an object that is flexible and changeable, but one that keeps its underlying structure even as it moves.[3] By thinking of the organization as adaptable in an uncertain environment, participants are more likely to consider more-creative strategies that allow the organization to plan for the unthinkable—major crises or radical changes in the environment.

Filters

For plot writers, the challenge may be in identifying and addressing staff attitudes that influence response to change. Behavioral theorists point out that managers filter information they receive to make an uncertain environment appear more certain. This behavior allows managers to simplify their view of reality and to decrease uncertainty so they can make decisions. Theorists have identified five information filters that have an impact upon managers' decision making:

- cognitive limits
- operational goals, incentives, and rewards
- information, communication, and measurement systems
- geographical and organizational structure
- culture, folklore, leadership, and tradition[4]

These filters can limit information that managers consider and limit the information they receive. For the scenario writer, these filters can limit what issues are considered or how data is viewed. Recognizing these filters, though, can open plot writers to a wide variety of information sources and can serve to remind scenario planners to look beyond the obvious in designing plausible scenarios.

Major Plot Lines

As noted in chapter 1, Schwartz has identified three major plot lines that apply to most situations: winners and losers, challenge and response, and evolution.[5] These story lines outline motivating forces of the main characters in the story. How these plots fit into a scenario planning process will depend on the driving forces identified in the planning sessions and on the focus or central elements considered to be most important and most uncertain.

Winners and Losers

In the winners and losers plot, resources are assumed to be scarce and conflict is an inevitable part of the scenes. Some groups will gain in this plot, some groups will lose. For example, if the scenario planning process is assessing how academic libraries will cope with rising serials prices in the future, one plot may describe a university where serials are supported by grant funds from academic departments. Those departments with major grants, usually in the sciences, would control serials expenditures. Humanities and social science departments with fewer grants would have fewer library resources. A result of such a situation would be the continued growth of science research and a subsequent decline in research activity in the humanities areas. The "haves" would control the research, the "have-nots" would become poorer and poorer. Such a plot if written from the viewpoint of a humanities faculty member, would be quite fatalistic, while the view from the science faculty members' perspective could be more optimistic. The story should be rich enough in detail, though, to help managers develop strategies to subsidize humanities research as well as to develop strategies to help move the humanities units from research endeavors to more pure teaching units. In any case, the plot gives the writers enough leeway to view a number of possible outcomes or end states for the story.

Challenge and Response

In the challenge and response plot, the organization faces a new challenge and designs a variety of responses. For libraries, technology presents a constant challenge. A challenge and response plot centering on emerging technologies could explore the scenarios of a library that chooses to be a cutting-edge institution experimenting with the newest technologies, a leading-edge institution adopting new but tested technologies, or a state-of-the-art institution that adopts proven technologies. Each of these responses yields a different future for an organization. Which story an organization chooses to develop will depend on how the political, economic, technological, and educational forces developed as part of the scenario planning process. The stories, though, should help decision makers assess the various responses to the challenge and then choose strategies that fit best with the perceived environment.

EVOLUTION

In the evolution plot, decision makers assume slow changes in trends that have an impact on the organization. Plots in this area may concentrate on changing demographics or a changing economic base for public institutions. For a library examining a changing population base, an evolutionary plot may be most appropriate. Changes in the age of the population served by a public library are likely to occur slowly, giving the library time to implement transition services to meet changing customer needs. Evolutionary trends are more easily managed than sudden shifts in the environment. As such, decision makers are generally more comfortable looking at issues that are seen as evolutionary rather than at issues that are more unpredictable.

Other Plots

Although the winners and losers, challenge and response, and evolutionary change are the most common plots found in scenario designs, other plots do surface in the discussion process.[6] Some of these plots may be more appropriate in the diverse, changing world of information technology and libraries.

REVOLUTION

In revolution plots, the decision makers describe radical changes and the impact those changes may have on the organization. For example, the widespread use of the World Wide Web has caused a revolution in how some people access information, what type of information is available, and who can access it. The questions of the library's role in providing access to the Internet, in protecting minors from accessing obscene material, and in incorporating the format into services are hotly debated and provide quite a lot of material for the scenario writer. Incorporating the revolution in Internet access into the plot lines of scenarios becomes a true challenge for organizational planners.

CYCLES

Another plot line is that of cycles: growth, development, and decline. This type of plot works well in looking at the economic future for public funding for public libraries or in looking at the impact of changing enrollments on higher education. Public and private organizations generally follow a cyclical growth pattern. Watching for the trend changes and composing plots to address these changes can be a useful exercise for library decision makers.

INFINITE POSSIBILITIES

A major optimistic plot line is that of infinite possibilities. Here resources are considered unlimited, growth is encouraged, and prosperity reigns. This plot line can be very uplifting. Still, writers of this plot line need to remember that some efforts can fail even in times of prosperity and growth. Achieving some reality in the plot line is likely to be the biggest challenge.

LONE RANGER

The Lone Ranger plot line emphasizes the individual against the system. Here the individual can be a unit of the institution that strikes out on its own or an organization that operates quite differently from others in the industry. For example, in viewing technological change and libraries, one plot could describe what happens when the computing support unit decides to go its own way and design systems that meet the "computing view" of the future. Or a plot could describe how a library could truly eliminate print resources as part of its services. The stories that are developed around the Lone Ranger plot line can help an organization identify potential conflicts within the organization, can help show where heros can become villains, and may help an organization design creative strategies to maximize the benefits of a Lone Ranger while offsetting the negative conflicts that develop.

My Generation

A final plot line is that of "my generation." This plot centers on how one's generation affects one's values and views of the environment and of the organization. These plots can help libraries design services to different groups or can help managers assess the impact of different groups on the work force. For example, a plot on library services needed in ten years for the baby boomer generation will yield one set of ideas, while a plot looking at youth services ten years from now may yield a very different set of needs and strategies. The challenge to decision makers is then to determine how to design transition services to meet changing needs of the population.

Writing the Script

Once the basic plot is outlined for the scenario, writers face the challenge of making the story plausible and entertaining. The story should be rich enough in details to provide decision makers with ideas of how the future could look while not becoming so detail oriented that the reader loses interest in the story. "By definition, a scenario is an outline of a plot: it should not be a complete script."[7] Writers must also try to balance short-term vision with long-range viewpoints. The story needs to be familiar enough that readers can relate to the elements in the story but still suspend their current visions of the organization to see the future from a new viewpoint.

Another temptation the writer needs to avoid is that of writing worst-case/best-case scenarios. Instead, each scenario should look at the future from a different perspective. The future is unlikely to be the average between good times and bad times. Scenarios should offer the reader plausible but different futures. The scenarios should not just be opposite ends of a single continuum.

Scenarios should also be internally consistent. The plot elements should fall together into a coherent tale. The plot should look at the future from a number of angles to be sure different reactions to change or to the driving forces are included.

Finally, it helps to give the scenarios distinctive names so that the readers can easily identify the key differences in the scenarios.

Catchy names can also help engage the readers' interest and motivate them to finish reading the plot.

Scenario writing needs to follow the elements of good storytelling. The scenario should have a plausible but intriguing plot, characters that capture the readers' imaginations, and a focus that is meaningful to the decision makers. Well-written stories will help advance the strategic planning and reflection process of the scenario development team. Poorly written stories may leave the team with little to use in their planning process.

Notes

1. Nicholas Georgantzas and William Acar, *Scenario-Driven Planning: Learning to Manage Strategic Uncertainty* (Westport, Conn.: Quorum Books, 1995), 62.
2. Georgantzas and Acar, 67.
3. Joan Giesecke, "Creativity and Innovation in an Organized Anarchy," *Journal of Library Administration* 14, no. 2 (1991): 69.
4. Georgantzas and Acar, 70.
5. Peter Schwartz, *The Art of the Long View; Planning for the Future in an Uncertain World* (New York: Currency Doubleday, 1991), 147–57.
6. Schwartz, 157–64.
7. Peter Schwartz, "Composing a Plot for Your Scenario," *Planning Review* 20, no. 3 (1992): 16.

4

Scenario Planning in the Learning Organization

JOAN GIESECKE
DEAN OF LIBRARIES
UNIVERSITY OF NEBRASKA–LINCOLN

Scenario planning, in addition to being a technique that asks managers to look beyond the obvious in planning future options, can assist units as they become learning organizations.

Scenario planning is a tool that can help managers move toward a learning organization because it promotes creative thinking by planners and a willingness to question assumptions and ask crucial questions about an uncertain future. Peter Schwartz, in "Using Scenarios to Navigate the Future," states, "the test of a good scenario is not whether it portrays the future accurately but whether it enables an organization to learn and adapt."[1] The skills that are essential for a successful scenario planning effort are also essential to the creation of a learning organization.

The Learning Organization

Why are organizations now seeking to become learning organizations? Why does this management strategy work in today's uncertain environment? Savvy managers are discovering that continuous learning or discovering new ways to accomplish the organization's goals is crucial to developing a successful continuous improvement program. The learning organization centers on the idea that promoting learning by staff encourages all staff to discover new ways to solve problems, discover new products, or propose new services that help the organization advance and meet its goals and objectives.

In a learning organization, creating knowledge and sharing that knowledge is done in an effort to improve work performance. If learning efforts do not result in work improvements, then learning has not occurred.

Peter Senge has identified five key principles or disciplines that can help organizations move toward becoming learning organizations. These are personal mastery, group learning, mental models, building shared vision, and system thinking.[2]

Personal mastery involves individual attitudes toward learning and learning organizations. Only individuals can learn, and if the individual members of the organization do not embrace the concepts of learning, then learning is unlikely to occur. Mental models look at the assumptions members of the organization use in making decisions and encompass all of the assumptions that people make about how the world operates and how the organization functions. In most organizations mental models are so ingrained that most staff are unaware of the models they use to function within the organization.

Group learning looks at how members of the organization share information. Group learning also focuses upon how members learn about how the organization functions.

A shared vision among members of an organization provides the framework for the organization to move toward becoming a learning organization. A shared vision that encompasses learning can help staff understand how the goals of the organization will help them grow as individuals and how they as individuals can in turn help the organization move toward its goals.

Systems thinking is the process of looking at the whole picture. It involves looking at how one part of the organization has an impact upon other parts of the organization.

While the concepts outlined by Senge provide a foundation for the discussion of learning organizations, the concepts are not specific enough to provide an action plan for managers to use in designing a learning organization. David Garvin, in his work on building learning organizations, points out that for the learning organization to become a meaningful concept for managers, three issues need to be resolved:

> A plausible, well-grounded definition of a learning organization is needed.
>
> Management strategies that can be operationalized need to be developed.
>
> The results of learning must be measurable to assess the impact on the organization.[3]

Addressing these three areas is crucial to the success of the learning organization movement.

Garvin provides an easy-to-apply definition of a learning organization. For Garvin, "a learning organization is an organization skilled at creating, acquiring, and transferring knowledge and insights."[4] He notes that this definition identifies the simple truth about learning in an organization. The organization must see a change in behaviors, processes, or work-related activities for learning to have occurred. Unless learning is applied in the work setting and is used to improve performance, the learning is not part of the overall learning-organization effort.

Second, Garvin identifies main activities or management strategies for the organization to use to begin building a learning organization. These reflect the overall disciplines outlined by Senge and form the basis for many total-quality-management (TQM) efforts. These activities are

> systematic problem solving
>
> experimentation with new approaches
>
> learning from their own experiences and past history
>
> learning from experiences and best practices of others
>
> transferring knowledge throughout the organization[5]

The transferring of knowledge throughout the organization is a key element of the learning organization and helps to distinguish learning-organization efforts from more traditional TQM programs. It is in sharing ideas and knowledge that staff can learn from each other. That learning can promote further improvement in the workplace.

Measuring learning is the third key aspect of the learning-organization processes. Many continuous-improvement and strategic-planning efforts concentrate on data gathering and analysis and measuring work processes. In the learning organization, measurement moves from just looking at data about work flow to examining how learning has occurred. Qualitative measures of employee efforts are needed to measure individual learning. Quantitative measures of cost reduction and process improvements help assess the outcome of learning efforts. To measure learning, then, qualitative, or soft, measures are needed along with analytical, quantitative efforts.

To build a learning organization, managers need to foster an environment that is conducive to learning, that allows for time for reflection and analysis, and that encourages sharing of ideas across organizational and unit boundaries. Tools to help managers achieve these objectives are needed if managers are to move beyond the theory and philosophy of the learning organization to apply the concepts to actual organizations. One such tool is scenario planning.

Scenario Planning and Learning

Scenario planning can assist managers in developing Senge's five disciplines within their own organizations.[6] Scenario planning can also help managers implement strategies proposed by Garvin for developing learning organizations. Because scenario planning does not concentrate on developing one vision or one future, the process is more flexible than traditional planning efforts and as such is more likely to promote learning. Like the process of becoming a learning organization, scenario planning is ongoing. Scenario planning also helps reinforce the connections among Senge's five disciplines in learning organizations and helps managers develop strategies for the future that can complement and enhance these disciplines.

Senge's Five Disciplines

PERSONAL MASTERY
Promotion of individual learning is the heart of the learning organization. Individual learning takes place as staff members recognize

the differences between the current state of the organization and the actions or strategies needed to move the organization toward its goals. This creative tension between the current reality and the vision of where the group wants to go leads to learning new skills, examining new procedures, and seeking actions that address future needs. With strategic-planning processes, the creative tension between current reality and the proposed vision for the future is evident in the process of identifying the critical success factors for the organization. These factors can be benchmarked against other organizations to identify best practices and options for the organization to pursue to meet its goals. The factors become part of the framework for developing strategies in the scenario planning process.

Scenario planning also promotes personal mastery by asking participants to think beyond their own view of the organization and to examine a variety of optional futures. Instead of just projecting historical trends into the future and assuming that the future will mirror the past, scenario planning helps individuals imagine different futures where trends from the past can change. Scenarios encourage staff to reframe their view of the future by freeing staff members' thinking from the present. Staff can then examine new futures from different perspectives and learn new ways to approach the creation of desirable futures for the organization. These exercises provide an opportunity to identify new skills staff will need in the future and to uncover core competencies that will be crucial for staff to meet if the organization is to move forward. Core competencies—skills, technical knowledge, and personal attributes—help staff members to successfully meet the future. Staff can also build strategies for the development of these skills into the scenarios and the scenario strategies. With several possible and plausible futures or scenarios, staff can work to develop their own competencies to meet anticipated future needs.

GROUP LEARNING

Working groups and teams are becoming the primary work unit in today's ever-changing organizations. Individual tasks and activities are being replaced by group efforts and team organizational structures. These work units promote a common understanding of the organization. Such organizational structures also require that members of the organization learn to interact and communicate clearly and effectively with each other. To do this, staff members must learn truly to listen to one another, to accept and respect each other as colleagues, and to be willing to learn from each other. These same skills are keys to a successful scenario planning session. Participants are expected to suspend their assumptions, creatively look to the future, design alternatives, and build on the ideas of other participants. They must be willing to listen and learn from each other. Scenario planning exercises then can help staff members hone their group-learning skills and improve their functioning as a work team. Additionally, scenario planning enhances institutional learning and helps to facilitate negotiation among managers, two skills very important to a learning organization.

Mental Models

It is perhaps in the area of identifying and attacking mental models that scenario planning can be most useful to a learning organization. Mental models are the assumptions and generalizations that influence how staff members understand and act within an organization. Members of the organization have their own ideas of how the organization functions and how variables in the environment act upon or have an impact on the organization. Managers will design strategies for action based on the assumptions they make about how the world operates.

To improve their ability to make decisions, managers need to become more aware of the assumptions they make and how those assumptions affect strategic variables. Unless managers find ways to explicitly identify these core assumptions, they are likely to make decisions and design strategies that assume that past trends will continue. Incremental change is likely to result when managers do not question their underlying assumptions. Although incremental change can be effective when the environment is relatively stable, incremental change is unlikely to help an organization anticipate discontinuities that can occur in an uncertain environment. Scenario planning helps staff members question these core assumptions. Scenarios can provide a forum for discussing assumptions and a vocabulary or language to address them.

Learning to identify mental models requires new skills from members of the organization. First, staff must learn to define key assumptions they hold about how the organization functions. Second, they must learn to be open to new ideas and strategies that question or attack these mental models.

Identifying mental models can cause great discomfort for staff. Many accepted principles and practices are not conducive to creating a different future. The ability to question these mental models, models that for many staff are accepted, ingrained, established, and not considered as anything but fact, may be very difficult. Staff must become comfortable with balancing inquiry that questions widely held assumptions with advocacy for a particular point of view, strategy, or even unit within the organization.

Staff need to develop skills for inquiry and skills for reflection. Inquiry skills are concerned with how staff interact with each other and how they deal with conflicting opinions and ideas. Reflection skills concern understanding leaps in abstraction or how individuals may reach or jump to conclusions about a particular idea or situation. Leaps in abstraction can be identified by asking what data are being used to reach a conclusion, what generalizations are being made, and what assumptions are forming the foundation for the idea. By testing conclusions, generalizations, and assumptions, the individual develops the needed reflection skills.

Advocacy skills need to be balanced with inquiry skills. Advocacy without inquiry leads to restricted "in the box" thinking. Asking a simple question, such as "Can you give me an example to explain your point?" can help break the reinforcing effects of confined advocacy thinking. Tactfully questioning another's idea or point of view by seeking further information rather than simply arguing a different viewpoint can yield a more-productive conversation and can promote learning. It can also help identify assumptions or mental models that are limiting the thinking of the individual or of the group.

Scenario planning efforts give individuals the opportunity to question beliefs and assumptions in a nonthreatening environment if participants enter the process with an open mind and a willingness to explore new ideas. The scenario planning structure provides a neutral framework for questioning current beliefs and efforts while structuring proposals to reach a new future for the organization. However, keeping an open mind may be one of the more difficult aspects of scenario planning for some staff members. It may be tempting for some to become particularly attached to a given scenario, particularly if that scenario reflects their own values and viewpoints. But, "scenario planning is not a crystal ball, no planning is."[7] Rather, the process encourages staff to examine more than one possible future. Encouraging staff to work on scenarios that do not reflect their own views or that make them uncomfortable can help staff break away from the mental models they hold about the world. In doing this they become more open to learning.

The skills that participants develop as part of the scenario planning process can transfer to the work setting and can provide individuals with tools to use to help attack mental models in other settings. This transfer of skills to the work setting, resulting in work improvements, helps learning occur and is a natural part of a learning organization. Through identifying and attacking current mental models, staff can begin to discuss mental models of the future.

BUILDING A SHARED FUTURE

The end product of a scenario planning exercise is a series of stories that describe plausible futures for the organization. These stories help staff make better decisions about the future and are used to develop strategies for the organization to meet its goals. The process of creating these stories allows members of the organization to participate in creating the future for the organization as well as developing a better understanding of where the organization is likely to go. The process helps staff develop a shared understanding of the organization and a shared vision of the organization. By developing and then adopting the proposed futures and using those as the basis for decision making, members of the organization develop a shared vision for the organization. This helps staff be better prepared for the uncertainties of the future and to prepare responses to future possibilities.

SYSTEMS THINKING

Systems thinking is essential to a learning organization. Members of a learning organization must understand how the parts of the organization fit together if they are going to be able to improve work processes and promote individual and organizational learning. For example, in libraries a strategy that benefits technical services operations may not be of equal value to public services units. A policy that makes decisions easier for front-line service personnel may wreak havoc on a technical processing procedure. An approach to problem solving that benefits a computer operation such as first in, first out, may or may not help other library units get timely, needed support. With systems thinking, staff learn to consider how a policy, procedure, or decision affects units outside their own. Staff need these same skills and insights in viewing strategy development as part of the scenario planning process. In scenario planning, members of the organization must look at how all parts of the organization are affected by a proposed future, by the strategies that are developed, and by the outcomes that are sought for each future option. Learning to think "outside the box," as participants develop alternatives that may be possible, helps participants think more broadly about the organization and, therefore, promotes systems thinking.

Garvin's Management Strategies

Scenario planning is also a useful tool in exploring the management strategies outlined by Garvin, particularly in the areas of experimentation and transferring of knowledge. Scenario planning encourages creative views of the future as part of the planning process. As such, it can help managers develop experiments to try as they develop strategies for coping with the various scenarios. But scenario planning is possibly most helpful in encouraging learning from others. Because scenario planning is a group process, participants are encouraged to look to others for ideas. Participants are also asked to look beyond their own experience to see the future from new perspectives. The process helps decrease defensive behaviors that arise when managers try to justify past actions in planning efforts and to move managers on to creating new futures. In such an effort, participants are well positioned to be open to learning and to apply that learning to the work setting. Finally, because scenario planning includes sharing the results of the planning process, that is, the stories that are developed, the process promotes the transfer of knowledge among units in the organization.

Learning for the Future

Scenario planning is one of many techniques that organizations can use as they move toward becoming a learning organization. The skills needed for successful scenario planning and the practice of those skills as part of the planning process will support the organization's efforts at learning. Recognizing those skills and promoting them as part of an overall organizational plan to encourage learning will go a long way in helping the organization move forward in an uncertain and changing environment.

Notes

1. Peter Schwartz, "Using Scenarios to Navigate the Future." Available online at http://www.gbn.org/Scenarios/Usingsp.html.
2. P. M. Senge and others, *The Fifth Discipline Fieldbook: Strategies and Tools for Building a Learning Organization* (New York: Currency Doubleday, 1994), 6–10.
3. David Garvin, "Building a Learning Organization," *Harvard Business Review* 78 (July/Aug. 1993): 78–91.
4. Garvin, 80.
5. Garvin, 81.
6. Thomas Charles, "Learning from Imagining the Years Ahead," *Planning Review* 22 (May/June 1994): 7.
7. Gordon C. Robbins, "Scenario Planning: A Strategic Alternative," *Public Management* 77 (Mar. 1995): 9.

Part Two

The Application

5

Arlington County Public Libraries Look to the Future

CATHY ROBINSON, ANDY CINCOTTA,
ROGER QUALTERS, AND ANN FRIEDMAN
ARLINGTON COUNTY PUBLIC LIBRARIES
ARLINGTON, VIRGINIA

Organizations plan for the future for many reasons. Often planning is a reaction to the multiple uncertainties of the present that are perceived to be escalating—world political unrest, rapidly changing technology, limited resources, or local community instability. Planning provides a level of control, a sense of what should be done to ensure the future of the service or organization.

The Arlington County Public Libraries, eight libraries strong with an annual budget of $8.5 million, exist in a world with all the pressures of a progressive urban environment as well as the stresses of a changing government culture. Government resources for non-mandated services are flat at best. Arlington is an urban county of 26 square miles, heavily dependent on a shrinking federal pres-

Acknowledgments: Library planning team members: Andy Cincotta, Elizabeth Cline, Carl Fisher, Carolyn Gershfeld, Lisbeth Goldberg, Ellen Hayes, Betty Horton, Kadija Lewally, Anne Lund, Jayne McQuade, Roger Qualters, Cathy Robinson; Marsha Allgeier, Department of Human Services, and Barbara Donnellan, acting director at the inception of the plan.

ence, with a resident population of 185,000 and a large daytime workforce that increases the population to 260,000. A large recent immigrant population in the school system places strong pressures on the county budget that are expected to continue well into the future. The Arlington County Public Libraries are a department of the county government with a county manager form of government. There is no library board; the director reports to the county manager.

In the face of a flat budget, the demand for traditional library services has not decreased. The residents annually visit the library an average of eight times per person and borrow an average of 10.4 items per person per year. Service to less-traditional library users in a county in which one in five residents is foreign born and one in four speaks a foreign language at home often demands more creativity, energy, and time than the library seems to have. Of course, global technology, of which many users are fully aware, has and will continue to transform information delivery and the public's perception of the library as an institution.

Beyond the external pressures, the county government is in the process of transforming itself into a high-performance organization (HPO). Not only is cost-effective, quality customer service the goal, but the pressure on departments (and the director) to redesign work in the spirit of the county's principles (high quality service, commitment to employees, empowerment, leadership, diversity, and teamwork) is very strong.

In the midst of this environment, an acting director and the library leadership team began the search for a planning methodology with strong hope that at least "direction," if not control and full funding, would flow from a planning effort. During this formative process of several months a new director was appointed—one with extensive planning experience and definite ideas on planning. From her experience, long-range planning was disappointing in both its process and the results of implementation. She felt long-range planning tends to not be bold enough and to be rooted in the past. Furthermore, it does not force one to let go of the current model of reality—even for a short period of time. Long-range planning does not allow for the possibility of a future that may be radically different from the present. She felt that a bolder and different approach was needed to produce a strong action plan and to jump start the culture change that was needed to move the organization toward HPO.

The director felt strongly that strategic plans/directions in some form should be the planning goal or the end product. Strategic directions are defined as "a pattern or a cluster of actions supported by policies, programs, decisions, and resource allocations that will bring substantial and sustainable benefits to the organization and will define what the organization is and what it does." However, the director also felt that before these strategic directions could be discussed, a *context*, or a story of several possible futures in which the strategies must operate, must be created. She stated:

> Our thinking needs to be liberated from the present to set the stage for bold action (or at least bolder action) than most public institutions ever contemplate or undertake.

Scenario planning became the methodology for creating the necessary context. It should be noted that the director was knowledgeable about scenario planning but had no direct experience in the scenario process.

The Planning Team

The library planning team (LPT) was composed of twelve individuals from all sections and levels of the library department. The members were selected by the library leadership team from a larger group that had been assembling all previous departmental planning documents and related information as well as exploring the pros and cons of various planning processes the department might undertake.

Accepting the Charge

The charge for the LPT was prepared by the library leadership team (LLT), then composed of the director, division chiefs, and the manager of the central library. The charge described the scenario planning process, defined the necessary products and timelines, emphasized the importance of making the principles of government an integral part of the process, and required that the entire organization be kept informed of and involved in the process. The charge stated that "all products should be short, cause us to do something differently, should be anchored in the future, and must fly 'in the hierarchy.'" The year 2010 was set as the scenario year—far enough in the future that it could not be reached without leaving the present.

Growing a Team

As the scenarios are not a long-range plan with specific goals and objectives, scenario planners do not need to be managers or to have managerial experience. However, staff working on scenarios need to possess good research and communication skills and have a sincere belief in the value of the project.

The Arlington team was initially self-nominated and very large. At the urging of the director and after the decision to go with the scenario process was made, the size of the team was reduced. Upper-management staff were asked to step down from the committee. The remaining members were given a choice on their continued participation. The twelve members who remained on the team were original members who chose to stay.

While research and communication skills varied, all members were committed to the project and worked hard to see it through. In the end, this dedication counted for more than research ability. However, a team of volunteers selected because they possessed the skills needed for a planning effort would have made work at the outset easier. It was impossible in this effort to do this; the volunteers were there, and they would serve.

Early in the process, team training or building was suggested. Because of the change in the team's membership and its direction, team members felt this was a needed step. Everyone participated in a full-day retreat in a state park about sixty miles from the library. A trained facilitator led the team through a series of physical exercises that emphasized the need for each individual's contributions to accomplish a group goal. Frustration, perspiration, and concentration helped individual members bond into a working unit. After the team-building exercise, the team returned to its charge with a new feeling of camaraderie and a heightened sense of humor.

To help ensure positive team interaction, ground rules were established and followed. Most important among these were that attendance at weekly meetings was compulsory and that the contents of meetings were confidential. "Say what you mean and mean what you say" was the by-rule of communication among team members. Every member agreed to participate but not dominate; the cochairs served as facilitators, coordinators, and coaches. It is important to note that all team decisions on initiatives were made by consensus, not by the cochairs. This method of operation is consistent with the county principles—and made manifest one of the culture changes necessary within the library.

Because scenario planning was a new concept for the team and the library, the playing field was level; there were no experts who felt they should have the leadership role. Leadership was exercised at different times by all members. For example, one team member took it upon herself to talk with staff from another county department who had done scenario planning the previous year. She read their documents and learned a great deal. She brought her newfound knowledge back and challenged the team to think independently of the existing charge, to propose a significant change to the team charge, and to seek assistance from staff with scenario planning experience in another county department. This initiative demonstrated the importance of each member's contribution in providing leadership to the team as a whole.

Revising the Charge

The library planning team contacted the department of human services (DHS), which had recently completed a scenario planning project. The DHS administrative division chief shared her experience and the scenario development philosophy and techniques learned from working with futurist/consultant Jay Ogilvy. This collaboration led to a revision of the LPT's charge and process. The original charge called for three or four scenarios from which one would be chosen as the most plausible. In addition, a narrative picture of the library operating as a high performance organization in that scenario was to be created.

After the discussion with someone who had completed a scenario planning process, it was decided that one scenario would not be singled out. This change would minimize the risk of appearing to predict the future, would increase flexibility in thinking, and would encourage those using the scenarios to look at multiple future possibilities. Also the integration of the concept of the library as a high performance organization was removed from the scenario process. It would occur at a later time through planning sessions of the library's extended management team. The director and the LLT readily accepted these changes. They too were willing to learn and change.

Scenario Planning Process

Preparatory research began with a review of the planning documents that had been collected. In the effort to open LPT members to alternative views of the future and important trends that might have a significant impact on Arlington, the team watched *Vision 2020,* a presentation of possible alternative futures for the county prepared by consultants David Snyder and Greg Edwards for the Arlington County Board. Exposure to these often unpopular views proved an effective catalyst for substantive discussion. Some of the videotapes from Joel Barker's *Discovering the Future* series were viewed at meetings to encourage team thinking "outside the box."[1]

Research Process

The team settled into a pragmatic work routine. Team members divided into five working subgroups, each charged with researching aspects of the library's environment: technology, the economy, the political climate, environmental factors, and social conditions. Subgroups reported back to the team as a whole. The team invited representatives from many county departments to its weekly meetings to report on various aspects of the county's policies, to reflect on their opinions of important trends, and to comment on the directions the county was taking. Participants included the heads of Management and Finance, Office of Technology and Information Services, and Economic Development and demographers from the Planning Division along with the chief of operations from the police department and the coordinator of school libraries. In addition, the team invited futurist Robert Olson, from the Institute of Alternative Futures, to provide his perspective, especially because he is an Arlington resident. From this discussion and previous research, the team created its first draft list of trends and factors believed to be of importance to Arlington County.

Research and writing skills varied among members. While all members chose to be on the team, contributions differed based on interest, abilities, and energy levels. Due to the extensive team-building work at the beginning of the process, this did not prove disruptive. All team members recognized the contributions of all others without regard to comparative achievements.

Developing the Scenarios

The final scenario logics evolved at a two-day session facilitated by the DHS chief. The team again retreated to facilities removed from the library environment. Away from library interruptions, the team began to debate the relative importance of the trends and factors identified in the research. Using a process based on that of Jay Ogilvy and of Peter Schwartz in *The Art of the Long View*, the set of trends and factors developed by the library planning team were analyzed, ranked, and grouped.[2] Figure 5.1 lists the ranking of factors that resulted from the LPT's efforts.

Figure 5.1 Arlington County Public Libraries Factor Ranking

1. Economy . . . . 31 points
   Cost of living, inflation, property values, tax base, cost of doing business, new businesses, employment/unemployment

2. Immigrant Population . . . . 15 points
   Origin, educational level, size of population, attitude of population toward government, aspirations, intention to stay, demand for materials, language

(Continued)

Figure 5.1 *(Continued)*

3. Government Decentralization................ 11 points
   Responsibility decentralized to states, to localities

4A. Legislation re: Telecommunications .... 9 points
    Cable, telephone, entertainment, encryption, copyright, ownership/monitoring/control of data

4B. Technological Changes..................... 9 points
    Expansion of technology, telecommunications, databases, shifting availability from print to electronic sources (related issues include pricing, availability, and the rapidity of change)

5A. Education .... 8 points
    Lifelong learning, retraining, partnerships with educational organizations, outsourcing/privatization, educational philosophy, home schooling, distance learning, literacy

5B. Reengineering, Redesign of Libraries .... 8 points
    Identify business goals, do more with less, competition—no longer public monopoly

6A. Household Income Level .... 7 points

6B. Changing Family Structure.................. 7 points
    Children, day care, single parent, nontraditional

6C. Employment/Unemployment .... 7 points
    How income is spent, welfare, need for information, where time is spent

6D. Disappearance of the Middle Class............ 7 points
    Income gap

6E. Printing and Publishing Industry.............. 7 points
    Paper prices, retooling, distribution methods, what is published, access to historical materials, electronic archival access

7A. Access to Information .... 6 points
    Who owns and controls, copyright, electronic sources, access to government information

7B.	Business Development	6 points
	Tax incentives, need to build business base	
8A.	Nontraditional Work/Education	5 points
	Telecommuting, distance learning, home schooling	
8B.	Attitude toward Government	5 points
	How big, level of tax support	
8C.	Format of Information	5 points
	Availability of general information, print–electronic	
8C.	Racial and Ethnic Polarization	5 points
9A.	Rise of Individualism	4 points
	Demand for service, right to service, customization of services, meet individual desires, need for access	
9B.	Diversity of Population	4 points
	Staffing that reflects community, broad view: age, lifestyle, ability/disability, cultural	
9C.	Low/No Commitment to Community Involvement. .	4 points
10A.	Downsizing–Retraining	3 points
	Retirees, migration	
10B.	Federal Deficit	3 points
	What level of government delivers a service, effect on patrons of spending changes	
11A.	Training of Staff	2 points
	Job skills, retraining, job obsolescence	
11B.	Role of Government in Social Values	2 points
	Censorship, control of access to information	
12A.	Customization of Information	1 point
12B.	Opting Out of Social Activities	1 point
	Single–issue advocacy, don't know neighbors	

After discussing the relative groupings of the factors, the team decided that the most important and most uncertain elements were economic factors and citizens' attitudes toward government and public goods. The team defined communitarian ideals as beliefs, held by people and their government, that value the inclusion of everyone in the political process, participation in community life, and provision of equality of opportunity. They then described the eroding middle class that results from the decrease in the number of middle-class people whose income is secure. Over the last fifteen years the median income has decreased 4.6 percent in constant, inflation-adjusted dollars. It is possible to have an eroding middle class in a strong or weak economy. The important element is the distribution of the gains: whether they are distributed in a way that permits the middle class to maintain its lifestyle or in a way that benefits only corporations and the rich and the inflation-adjusted income of the middle class declines. The socioeconomic forces and citizens' attitudes became the axes of a matrix around which the scenarios were built. (See figure 5.2.)

Using all of the information that had been collected, the team considered the probable impact of relevant trends and factors and brainstormed the elements for one of the scenarios. After this

Figure 5.2 Arlington County Public Libraries Matrix of Most-Important Elements

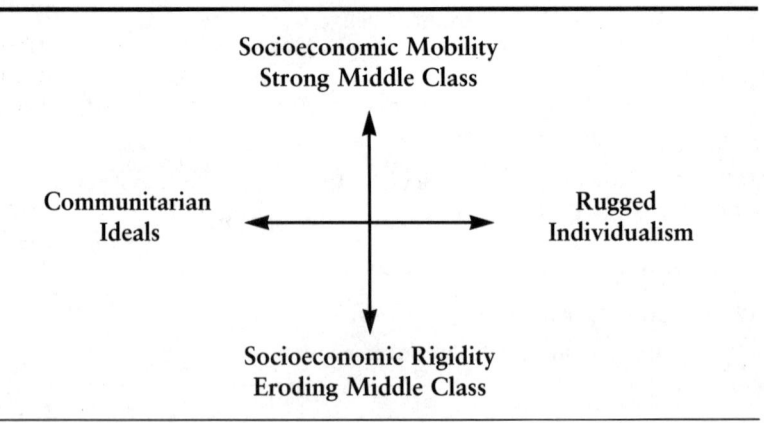

```
                    Socioeconomic Mobility
                    Strong Middle Class
                              ▲
                              │
    Communitarian    ◄────────┼────────►    Rugged
    Ideals                    │             Individualism
                              │
                              ▼
                    Socioeconomic Rigidity
                    Eroding Middle Class
```

group experience, the team broke into three subgroups to brainstorm the elements for each of the other scenarios. Benefiting from the experience and leadership of the DHS chief, individual concerns and tensions dissipated, and all team members were candid, humorous, and productive through the entire process.

For continuity in writing, the LPT cochairs were selected by the team to write the actual scenarios. Finally, the written scenarios were submitted to the entire library planning team as well as the library leadership team for comment.

The scenarios were written at the extreme points of the matrix to accentuate differences and were given imaginative titles to facilitate discussion. The manner in which influencing factors would play out in a quadrant controlled the logic of the story. The creative writing could have continued indefinitely, but after many iterations over three weeks, the team (and the director) said "good enough"; these scenarios were not the "truth" and they did not have to be "perfect."

Four scenarios were developed from the matrix. (See figure 5.3.) See the appendix at the end of this chapter for the scenario stories.

Communicating the Process

Even the best-written scenarios have little impact if the organization as a whole does not buy into the process and understand and "feel" what it might be like to live in the futures that are described. At each step along the way, the planning team strove to involve staff. It was evident that when people were caught up in day-to-day task work, it was hard to think about possible futures and to plan for them. In the beginning, the effort to reach all levels of staff was an uphill struggle.

The team published a biweekly newsletter, *The Stargazer Gazette*, that reported on the team's activities and encouraged readers to respond or contribute. Copies were sent to each unit within the library. Cartoons and interviews submitted by staff members were published and provocative articles that the team found were summarized. In its final issues, the *Gazette* published capsulized versions of the scenarios as a way to introduce the stories to those who had avoided reading the complete report distributed earlier. Articles

Figure 5.3 Arlington County Public Libraries Scenario Matrix

Socioeconomic Mobility
Strong Middle Class

All American Arlington (AAA)	*Proposition 13*
Strong economy	Strong economy
Much opportunity for upward mobility	Much opportunity for upward mobility
A middle class that values the inclusion of everyone in community life and believes in equality of opportunity for all	A middle class that values self-determination and minimal government interference

Communitarian Ideals ←——————→ **Rugged Individualism**

Alice's Restaurant	*Let Them Eat Cake*
Weak economy	Strong economy
Limited opportunity for upward mobility	Limited opportunity for upward mobility
A middle class that has lost significant ground economically and that values the inclusion of everyone in community life and believes in equality of opportunity for all	A middle class that has lost significant ground economically while the rich grew richer and that values self-determination and minimal government interference

Socioeconomic Rigidity
Eroding Middle Class

---

were also included in the library's newsletters. Progress reports were made at management team meetings throughout the project.

Team members attended the staff meetings of all library units to report and invite feedback on the planning process. Responses to these visits ranged from skepticism or silence to lively, productive participation.

It was essential that the planning effort engage members of the library's management group. Two meetings of the library's extended management team, a group that includes branch managers and unit supervisors, were held. At each meeting a progress report was delivered and feedback invited. The information was politely received, but little concrete feedback was generated. The director, though not a member of the LPT, stayed closely in touch throughout the process.

Presenting the Product

The window of opportunity for staff participation in the process was the annual all-staff-day program. Once a year the library system closes to the public for employee training and morale/team building. All staff attend a morning training program and are provided a selection of afternoon training sessions. The morning session was devoted to the scenario process.

Members of the library planning team, the library director, and futurist Robert Olson planned the program. Olson and the DHS division chief began by providing a short explanation of the value and uses of scenario planning and a description of the process the LPT had used.

Scenario depictions in the form of tableaux performed by LPT members and staff volunteers were followed by a small-group exercise. The intent of this exercise was to have individuals imagine a possible future by getting actively involved in what life might be like in a particular scenario. This was also an opportunity to lend some humor and enjoyment to the process so it could move beyond the realm of management theory. After the scenario immersion, the groups had a chance to protest conditions in the scenario by identifying a reason to picket the library. After choosing a protest slogan and a rally chant, they created a picket sign and returned to the library's auditorium where each group could "demonstrate." For a few minutes, vocal outcries were heard and the message was clear that All American Arlington was the scenario of choice.

Although in scenario planning an organization does not choose a preferred scenario, the activity of protesting against a scenario proved immensely successful for a variety of reasons. First, it was fun. While individual staff members resisted the reality of some of the scenarios and certainly did not want to live in most of these futures, being encouraged to protest what the library had become in these futures allowed an element of playfulness to enter the picture. The diverse composition of the team increased the trust and participation of staff in the day's activities and helped to communicate the message.

Evaluating the Process

Throughout the scenario planning process, feedback from staff was encouraged. Verbal, written, or electronic reaction was requested in virtually every communication from the LPT. Evaluation forms were used both at the extended management team meeting and at all staff day. While staff-initiated communication with the LPT was limited, evaluation instruments were well used, and the feedback indicated overall satisfaction. The written evaluation distributed at all staff day indicated that 93 percent had at least an adequate understanding of the scenario planning process and the scenarios that were presented.

Moving Forward

After the completion of the scenarios and the presentation to staff, the next step was to determine what strategic directions or actions, if begun today, would have substantial and sustainable benefits in any or all of the futures described in the scenarios. This discussion and direction setting was considered more appropriate for library management than for the LPT. Two meetings of the extended management team were scheduled during the quarter following all staff day. In addition to the usual participants, the director selected members of the planning team to take part in these sessions.

In preparation for the first meeting, participants were divided into four groups. Each group met, imagined itself in one scenario, and from the context of that scenario produced a list of key three- to five-year strategic directions that would maximize the library's potential within its confines. Then the groups convened as a whole and the four lists were compared and merged. Comparison showed some strategies would be effective in all or at least three scenarios. Those strategies or strategic directions were captured as directions that would be most productive for the library to pursue. The three strategic directions, with a little editorial massaging that occurred later in the LLT, are

1. Exploit technology appropriately, efficiently, and effectively to provide what customers want.
2. Redesign work and provide continuous training for staff and volunteers to achieve higher customer satisfaction and ensure that more customers' needs are met.
3. Aggressively maintain and pursue strong and diverse funding.

The scenarios had liberated and forced more energy than the library culture in Arlington would have produced without the presentation of the dramatic futures. Technology is to be "exploited" for the benefit of customers. Work should be designed so customers are satisfied. To achieve this high level of customer satisfaction, staff deserve continuous training. And to make this all work, the library must be aggressive about all funding. The planners and the organization as a whole could see that these actions/directions would produce concrete benefits if aggressively pursued—and strong words were used to express what needed to be done.

Vision and Mission

The vision and mission statements are usually the first two documents created in a comprehensive-planning process. We did them last. Over the years Arlington County and its library system have developed and articulated many principles, visions, and missions. Revisiting them at the beginning of the process would have started a conversation that the director felt would have produced little new thinking but certainly would have produced months of discernment—and ultimately frustration as the precise words to describe our best selves and that of our organization were sought.

Consequently, at the end of the planning cycle the library leadership team was joined by some members of the planning team and a few staff "learning partners," who were selected for their "big picture" perspective and diversity, to create the vision and mission statements. Provided with the scenarios and the strategic actions, team members, within a two-hour period, easily created vision and mission statements that aligned and unified the whole planning process:

Vision: As we enter the twenty-first century, we are committed to building community and to being Arlington County's gateway to the pleasure of reading and to information

- for every Arlingtonian
- on any subject
- in many formats
- at any time

To achieve this end, our energy and efforts will be far-reaching, diversified, and multifaceted.

Mission: The Arlington County Public Library

- provides access to information
- creates connections to knowledge
- promotes the joy of reading

Proceeding toward the Future

Where do we go from here? The scenarios need to be revisited periodically and corrected as new information is available. For example, what will be the effect of welfare reform and the new immigration laws on Arlington's future? We need to make the scenarios come alive for the leadership team when strategic directions are reviewed and annual work plans are written and evaluated. Most importantly, the leadership must remember (and revisit) these futures and consider the impact of the strategic directions. The question must be asked often: Is what we are doing creating substantial and sustainable benefits for the future? Only by testing planned actions against this question are we likely to stay on target and prosper. Strategic directions must help us choose to do one thing over another with the confidence that it is the right action.

Achievements and Lessons Learned

In the year since the strategic directions were completed, what has been accomplished? A new information system is about to come online. This system is innovative and progressive and moves the library about ten years ahead of its previous system. The implementation of the system has been accompanied by an aggressive training program for all staff using a train-the-trainer approach. This system, costing more than $1 million, has been funded by county government in an era of flat budgets. Work redesign has accompanied the technological changes: An entire division has been restructured, and a full technology support unit has been created. Public service staff are beginning to integrate the concept of nonmediated service and remote access. Empowerment and leadership of all staff are becoming more the norm in the changing culture. Finally, a library materials endowment has begun with the goal of raising $1 million over five years.

Did all of this happen only because of the scenarios and the strategic directions? No, the fact that the time was right for a lot of these changes helped. The strategic directions energized the effort. We knew we were on the right track. Also the changes helped jump start the culture changes that are needed to support a principled, high-performance effort. Most importantly, the scenarios built on our institutional and cultural tendency to believe and enjoy story experiences, and they gave us time to internalize the facts that the future was going to be totally unlike the past and that we as an institution better do something to meet it proactively if we wished to remain viable. Without the scenarios we would never have confronted and believed this reality.

What did we do right, and what would we do differently if we could do it all again? The following lists include a few lessons learned.

Beginnings

In deciding whether to use scenario planning, it is important to consider your community: Will your world see or care about your plan? What is your community's current knowledge and response to scenario planning? If the public is involved, the scenarios will be less bold. And rejection of certain scenarios as politically untenable and even unspeakable is a real possibility. Be prepared for it! No one in Arlington will admit that Alice's Restaurant is a possibility—or will run for political office on that possibility!

- Public libraries have a very strong story experience—scenarios use this experience well.
- Public libraries and librarians will buy the story approach to planning, but it must be communicated to all staff during the process again and again. Established communication channels must be used—new channels must be found.
- The scenario process has to be fun to be effective. Take the time to make it so.
- The scenario building process needs a champion. The director must track the process and become one of its active champions.
- If you get involved with futurists, make sure they are rooted in reality—at least somebody's reality that you can identify.
- Remember "the fly in the hierarchy" rule. Planning methodology and products must be acceptable to the hierarchy to have any long-term effect at all. An unacceptable, visionary, bold plan is worthless.

Making It So

- A planning process should not be undertaken until permanent organizational leadership is in place. Planning requires stability and a sure direction at the top of the organization.
- Key factors, such as the size and composition of the team and the charge, should be decided upon early—and the direction should be sustained if at all possible. It is difficult to explain changes of direction as anything but "they don't know what they are doing."
- Set a timetable for the completion of the tasks and stick to it. Six to seven months is enough time to create acceptable scenarios.
- In selecting team members, find staff who are willing to start with a belief that the future will be different from the present—and perhaps totally unlike the present.
- Attend to the development of team skills. It is useful to bring in a trained facilitator whenever possible. A facilitator who has experienced the process and can help direct it can increase participant confidence and reduce tension.

Strategic Directions

Strategic planning can be accomplished in three months after the scenarios are completed.

The team that created the scenarios most likely will not be the team that will do the strategic thinking. This is a management function.

If your management team is not sufficiently diverse, seek learning partners from within the organization for the activity.

The strategic planning should focus on the three- to five-year future—not the fifteen-year horizon of the scenarios.

There tends to be no consensus in the electorate on the services to be provided. This makes choosing strategic directions, rather than specific strategic actions, more beneficial in the long run. It gives the institution options and flexibility and avoids "popular" choices that will not have the desired impact.

The strategic directions should energize staff and indicate one action over another.

The number of directions or actions should range from three to five—and their descriptions be kept to about ten words.

If the strategic directions are to have an impact, the director should be able to remember them easily without notes and use them frequently in talking about the organization and its future. Such familiarity and use of the strategic directions gives them urgency and importance.

The implications and impact of what is created by the strategic directions is generally far greater than what anyone might anticipate.

The Final Phase

Another look at the institution's existing vision and mission statements for alignment with the new strategic directions can be productive at the end of the process.

Annual system and unit work plans that carry out the strategic directions are a must.

In conclusion, we learned not to try to get the model absolutely right, particularly when trying to do this without ongoing consultant help. Be raggedy; it will still work. You can recover from missteps as long as there is a good attitude and goodwill on the part of the participants and the director. We lost our way several times and recovered.

Brian Quinn of Dartmouth has said that "a good deal of organizational planning . . . is like a ritual rain dance. It has no effect on the weather that follows. . . . Much of the advice related to planning is directed at improving the dancing, not the weather."[3] This cannot be said of scenario planning. The energy and direction realized by our process and product has improved the "weather" for the Arlington Public Libraries.

Notes

1. Joel Barker: Discovering the Future Series, *The Business of Paradigms*, 38 min., 1989; *The Power of Vision*, 30 min., 1991; *Paradigm Pioneers*, 30 min., 1993 (Burnsville, Minn.: Chart House), videocassettes.
2. Peter Schwartz, *The Art of the Long View: Planning for the Future in an Uncertain World* (New York: Currency Doubleday, 1991).
3. James Brian Quinn, *Strategies for Change: Logical Incrementalism* (Homewood, Ill.: Irwin, 1980), 122.

APPENDIX

Scenario Stories

All American Arlington (AAA)

Communitarian ideals, including the belief that government intervention in social and economic programs is desirable and effective, are held by the majority. The knowledge that hard work will lead to success and upward mobility revived the middle-class American dream.

The steady decrease in the national debt after the tax reforms of the late 1990s and the trade turnaround following the removal of trade barriers and the restoration of stability after the dissolution of the Soviet Union have led to a world market open to business and innovation as well as a consistently positive U.S. balance of trade. The U.S. economy was well poised to profit from the products of the twenty-first century: arbitrage, computers, cinema, CDs, and cable television. An enlightened entrepreneurial spirit has revitalized American business and led to the creation of enough high-value jobs to make middle-class hopes for a better future realistic. Following the example of Coca-Cola and McDonald's, there are now Price Clubs in Havana and Club Meds in Afghanistan. The spread of American business and culture has brought mixed blessings to the world, however. The desire for things American and the adoption of a more materialistic, consumer-oriented culture has caused resentment and anti-American backlash among the traditional and religious members of these societies.

With the national debt reduced, the downsizing of the federal government accomplished, and social programs narrowly defined, states and localities had to take responsibility for programs or such programs ended. The result was a very limited safety net and large inequities between rich and poor areas. Without tax incentives for cultural or charitable contributions, whim, ego, propaganda value, and occasionally conscience were the motives for philanthropic giving, and that spent on social needs did not go far. Eventually, mass protests over the inequities led to social turmoil and a growing awareness of a gross imbalance in the distribution of wealth. The national mood began to swing back toward a stronger federal presence in the social fabric of the country. In the most-recent election, the nation has returned to the White House an activist President and a Congress dominated by progressive leadership willing to reconstruct some portion of the safety net of the past. The "new" politics lean toward privatization of government-funded services with strong federal oversight.

Technological advances, especially in telecommunications and information storage and retrieval, have shrunk global distances, making the entire world one marketplace. Highly qualified individuals of all nations move freely among positions in multinational corporations, often changing national residence for a period of years.

Biomedical technologies have contributed greatly to the length and quality of human life. In the United States, basic national health care has become a necessity. Technological advances in genetic engineering and other expensive high-tech treatments are available, however, only to those who can afford them. Other new and costly technologies have improved the physical environment of the United States, but elsewhere development and the profit motive coupled with the lack of government oversight have resulted in a deteriorating global ecology.

As free trade, stability, and economic opportunity increased globally, the impetus for large-scale immigration declined. The increase in positive business relationships and reduction in competition for economic opportunities reduced class and cultural friction in the United States. Most of the immigrants of the 1980s and 1990s have stayed in the United States and increasingly participate in daily life while maintaining their own cultural identity. For many, their country of origin has changed beyond recognition, and their children, born in the United States and carrying U.S. citizenship, have no desire to "return" to a land in which they had never lived.

In Arlington County, local government is in tune with the progressive federal government. Board members see the county government as a partner with community agencies in the provision of services in the public interest. An attitude of cooperation and optimism supports community services. Participation in religious groups and their social activities has increased. Members are an important source of community-project volunteers, and their work together on projects has increased understanding between groups. The local church council has strongly supported the library in the few censorship issues that have arisen. The Arlington Community Foundation has achieved its goal three years running, with corporate donations outpacing private two to one.

New international businesses choose to locate their headquarters in Arlington because of its proximity to Congress and federal agencies, the general quality of life, and the highly skilled labor pool. While advanced technologies allow telecommuting, teleconferencing, and remote access, many companies have continued to feel the advantages of face-to-face contact with federal officials. Moreover, the competition for federal dollars is so keen that many companies fear losing out by not creating personal relationships with their federal counterparts. These businesses support a large commercial real estate base and broad tax base, which ensures a relatively stable county budget. County services include increased neighborhood services, increased per capita student spending, and increased library and recreational services. The national decrease in immigration has led to a parallel decrease in Arlington's immigrants and a more-stable population. Continuing support for neighborhood services, human services, and education has paved the way for increasing participation of immigrant populations. This support has decreased racial and ethnic polarization and resentment of entitlements. Entitlements are fewer and extended for shorter lengths of time than in the past as the possibilities for upward mobility increase for everyone.

The Arlington populace has come to expect efficiently provided, top-quality services from the county government. Attaining this has involved a period of downsizing Arlington government and the elimination or privatization of some former county services. Arlington is seen as a community that demands good value for its tax dollar and prides itself on this point. Citizens are somewhat smug in their insistence that an efficient and effective community can provide extensive, high-quality services. The county's reputation as a county with strong citizen participation has attracted residents with long-term goals and aspirations. Arlington's redeveloped housing stock has drawn young families, the newly retired, and upwardly mobile singles. Arlington leads the metropolitan area in promoting, through the Metropolitan Area Council of Governments, a regional approach to common needs and problems, such as transportation, parks, and health services.

The library has kept up with the demand for high-tech services and continues to provide traditional library services. The governmental role has expanded to the extent that the library is perceived as an essential part of government and a catalyst for bringing parts of the community together.

Proposition 13

The breakup of the Soviet Union and the subsequent defeat of communism as a competing economic model have left the United States with a sense of self-confidence and assurance unparalleled since the end of World War II. Laissez-faire government policy toward business has been highly successful in ensuring that U.S. dominated corporations increase their global market share. Only a low flat income tax and small national sales tax are needed to continue paying off the national debt and finance the downsized federal government and programs. Business has responded with enthusiasm in this environment, developing new market frontiers in third world and formerly communist societies and creating high-value jobs for Americans. Bigger is again better. Major gains in productivity, fueled by the maturing technology and information revolution as well as new international markets and unfettered trade, permit high levels of economic activity throughout the economy. Sufficient high-value jobs have been created to stabilize and strengthen the economic basis of the middle class. Controlled immigration ensures the availability of an adequate number of lower paying jobs for blue-collar citizens.

This strong economic base, providing individual opportunity for those who apply themselves, has promoted a renewed faith in the efficacy of self-determination and strong middle-class values. The economic reward is all the sweeter as individuals do not feel penalized for earning more. There is a widespread determination not to make the mistakes of the past by investing in large social programs that enable the poor to subsist yet do not solve the problem of poverty. There is little faith in the ability of government to effect social change, but renewed faith in the ability of the individual to control his own destiny. The government that interferes least is best, and many services formerly provided by government are now provided by private, profit-making companies or are contracted for by the government. For example, federal park lands, while still owned by the federal government, are managed by conservation companies that contract out food and lodging facilities. Most notable, the Grand Canyon is now managed by Walt Disney, Inc., and combines high-quality food, lodging, theme park areas, and a multiacre shopping mall.

The expectation that people have responsibility for their actions and the downsizing of public assistance programs has made life much tougher for those who relied upon them. One benefit accruing from this attitude (and the enormous capabilities of the technological information network) is that no one escapes financial responsibilities such as child support unless he or she opts out of society completely. Civil libertarians have a number of suits pending on privacy rights as well as on the possible excessive influence on political matters by church groups with political agendas.

The general infrastructure is well maintained. Adequate utilities and good transportation are essential to the smooth functioning of business. There are minimal government interferences in social issues and few entitlement programs. Environmental protection is paid lip service. Regulatory agencies have diminished roles. Much of the responsibility for first-line inspection has been delegated to the company. Responsibility for social welfare that the federal government formerly provided is now contracted out to private or nonprofit organizations. For example, when the Mississippi floods, the Red Cross responds and may be given federal funding, but there is no longer a Federal Emergency Management Administration. This arrangement frees individuals to choose to participate at a community level in local charities and fund-raising events. The falloff in charitable giving following the tax code revision has not improved the ability of charities to provide a temporary safety net for local citizens in need. Givers, particularly corporate ones, expect a lot in return for their money. Individual philanthropic acts tend to fund the interests of the givers.

Arlington County's diverse residents have eagerly joined in the national business revival. Business boosters who believe in low taxes and privatized government services dominate the county board. Their first concern about any action or policy is the effect it will have on the business climate. The number of employees overseeing contracts has increased as the number providing any direct service diminished. The personal property and business license taxes have been abolished. Arlington businesses, with ample technical and technological resources including consultant and business services, have flourished. Pervasive technology has radically altered the way business relates to the consumer. The work environment for many no longer involves a specific geographic location or group of coworkers; work groups are put together on an as-needed basis by project managers. Customization of services and the shifts in the way consumers get information have led to bankruptcy for many "old-fashioned" companies that did not move with the times.

Arlington government has removed itself from the "business" of owning and operating summer camps for kids and swimming pools for adults and families; these services are provided by profit-making companies. People without adequate resources may apply for limited assistance from public or private sources, but most go without. Shelters for the homeless are a relic of the past. Families are expected to provide for their own, and public homelessness, like public drunkenness, leaves one open to arrest. Initially, this policy led to overcrowding in jails, but when privatized jails were permitted to use social-problem detainees as unpaid labor, jail became a less-appealing option, and former inmates tended to vote with their feet by moving to isolated rural areas where apprehension is less likely. There is concern about the size of some of the areas where large numbers of disturbed or lawless vagrants abide.

Believing that a better life is possible through better education, there is a strong demand for high-quality public education. Students, parents, and teachers are accountable for ensuring that education is effective. There is an expectation that students who want a higher education will successfully apply themselves to their studies. Following middle school, those with proven academic ability may continue to higher education and those who choose to, or who cannot compete, receive job training. At age 16, trainees who choose not to apply themselves are no longer part of the public education system and are on their own. Arlington competes nationally for the most highly qualified teachers, and prides itself on a school system in which 85 percent of those graduated continue their academic education. Most of those in job training complete their studies and find good jobs in a solid job market. Those who drop out must rely on their families for assistance or find whatever job they might be able to do. Members of the lower socioeconomic groups make up the bulk of this group.

Though the library is supported as an educational institution that helps people help themselves, the lower level of funding for all government service necessitates a redefinition of services and personnel requirements.

Alice's Restaurant

The Balkanization of the world following the breakup of the Soviet Union has led to a disruption of commerce and stagnation in global economic growth. Regional wars, a weak United Nations, and isolationist foreign policies have gutted trade policies such as GATT and NAFTA, making foreign investment problematic. The United States nearly fell victim to the same forces when the disastrous attempt to balance the budget and reform the tax code led to such an inequitable and unstable condition that wide-scale rioting was only narrowly avoided. With the "new focus" on domestic needs, expenditures on the military and foreign aid have been cut to the bone, permitting our limited resources to be used for domestic purposes.

With the "new commitment" to communitarian ideals, we value everyone's participation in the political process and in community life and understand the importance of equality of opportunity in our diverse and healing society. The need for effective social and economic government programs is great, though with enormous deficit spending and high inflation. Even with the addition of the peace dividend to the domestic economy and higher taxes, it has become increasingly difficult to pay for such programs. The government oversees and funds social programs such as job retraining and the provision of basic needs. The national health program is plagued by cost overruns, and there are questions about its viability. Still, national health care, social security, and low-cost student loans are considered essential government services.

Legal immigration has been legislated to an all-time low, and most government services can be provided only to citizens. Individual income taxes are at an all-time high, but there are tax incentives to stimulate business, particularly high-tech business. Inflation is a problem, though in an ironic way it is also helping in the effort to reduce the national debt by making the money we repay the debt with "cheaper." Though the minimum wage has been raised twice in five years, it is not keeping pace, and middle/lower incomes continue to slip.

Widespread application of technologies in education and service industries has provided an effective way to deliver services with considerably less human intervention and travel. Electronic classrooms, for example, permit more-efficient use of teachers and classroom space, with many students able to complete much of their studies off site or from home through use of interactive telecommunications.

The Arlington County Board has been reelected with the mandate to spend its resources as equitably and efficiently as possible. There is considerable civic pride in the degree of interpersonal acceptance and assistance displayed by Arlingtonians, particularly in such economically trying times when the natural tendency is to find scapegoats. Criticism by the Taxpayers Alliance, while politely received, rarely results in significant cuts because the human needs of residents have priority. The same is true of the advice provided by a few small church groups who reject communitarian ideals on moral grounds.

A wide variety of traditional government services, such as job training, basic educational skills for adults, vouchers for food, health care, transportation, and information services are provided in partnership with many community and private organizations. So far partnerships have succeeded in providing a safety net for Arlington citizens, many of whom are underemployed or unemployed.

The library has formed partnerships with many nonprofit, for-profit, and regional organizations to provide the access, materials, and services the community needs. Student volunteers from high schools and colleges provide much assistance at libraries and other public institutions as a way to "give back" something to their community.

There is strong community commitment, with "habitat for humanity" type organizations cleaning up neighborhoods, renovating old houses, and building new ones. The philanthropic donations of the wealthy to the Arlington Community Foundation have often made the difference in the economic viability of numerous community services.

County residents support a "business friendly" community and infrastructure. Though attracting and maintaining businesses is essential to avoid even higher unemployment, the impact on the environmental quality of life is still a consideration. Parks and outdoor recreation are important and maintained by those who use or live near them. Though much of the once important import/export industry was lost, the county succeeded in maintaining a relatively strong professional and service industry base as well as keeping lobbyists, associations, and telecommunication companies. Many residents who work for these companies volunteer their professional services and labor for important community projects. The Chamber of Commerce plays a leading role in the business-to-business selling of Arlington as a good choice.

Library services are important, and the library is viewed as an essential part of government as well as a catalyst for bringing the community together. Its popularity may also be due to the fact that it is a traditionally middle-class institution offering free "entertainment" to a group that remains socially middle class but is strapped by declining real wages, high taxes, high inflation, and little prospect for a brighter economic future. Inexpensive telecommunications make access to business and government, including libraries, easier.

Let Them Eat Cake

The global economy is highly complex with entangling GATT and NAFTA-type treaties. With the successful application of technology, corporations are larger, more efficient, and able to operate with fewer, lower paid employees. The military industrial complex has been replaced by a political industrial complex, out of touch with the ordinary citizen. Corporate influence in the political arena can be seen in the reduction and privatization of regulatory and government service agencies of every kind. There is little enforcement of what federal environmental legislation is left, and companies often pollute when they can get away with it; environmental action is local. The budget cutting mindset of the mid-1990s has been maintained, and federal and local governments have continually downsized. The budget is balanced, inflation and unemployment are low, and the income tax is flat. Because of low wages, individuals often work a second part-time job. Of necessity, virtually all women and most teenagers do some type of work and must contribute to the family income.

Capitalism has proceeded unabated as the global economic model. Multinational corporations move to increase their wealth at a dizzying pace, reducing their payrolls even in times of large profits. There is little company commitment to employees and less employee loyalty toward companies. Economic indicators continue to indicate growth while salaries for middle-class blue- and white-collar jobs are stagnant or decreasing due to the availability of a large qualified labor pool. Corporations, benefiting from a large labor pool, support high immigration quotas. Immigrants continue to come to the United States. The standard of living is decreasing, but it is still higher than in other countries. Many immigrants lack basic skills needed to rise above the most menial jobs and often contribute to the ghetto underclass. The government takes no leadership role in this situation.

With positive economic indicators, highly paid politicians and policymakers share a sense of pride in the progress of the economy. The reality is that the middle class is disappearing and with it many middle-class values. People are bitter as they see unbridled greed among the rich and the multinational corporations while their own slice of the pie shrinks. With no tax breaks for charitable giving, corporate dollars migrate toward political action committees rather than charities. The rich have little contact with the rest of society; "out of sight, out of mind" might be the assessment of their level of interest in those outside their circle. Average citizens do not understand the economic issues and feel helpless in the situation. They have lost faith in the ability of the government or any politician to improve things and believe that they can rely only on themselves, their family, and friends. Entitlement programs are viewed as big-government/high-tax bureaucracies that destroy the work ethic. In this self-reliant political atmosphere, such programs have been reduced or eliminated. In the absence of government safety nets, the extended family has become very important and more self-sufficient.

Political action is highly fragmented. Individuals coalesce around single issues, and groups dissolve upon the resolution of issues. NIMBYism ("not in my backyard!") is alive and well. People tend to be swayed by whatever populist candidate has promised to support the issue in which they are currently most interested. While the popular thinking is that the government that governs least governs best, citizens expect the local government to "enforce" their moral codes. Mainstream sentiment is that the federal government should not intrude in the daily lives of citizens to "legislate morality," but fundamentalist interest groups have succeeded locally in achieving government oversight of school curricula, textbooks, and public library materials.

The Arlington County Board is a mix of conservative budget cutters and a few old-time-party community leaders. The once dominant Arlington middle class is now in the minority. The area economies were unable to recover from the loss of so much federal employee income following the downsizing. Former federal employees who took early retirement during the first rounds of budget cutting have now become the frail elderly. With shrinking pensions, little public health care, and no government safety net, they depend financially on family and friends. Those who could leave have left Arlington to live with family in other parts of the country. Those who could not leave live in near poverty.

There is polarization between social classes, between ethnic and racial groups, and between socioeconomic groups. Churches and small charitable organizations with dwindling memberships try to bridge the economic gap, but individual frustration often results in feelings of anger and alienation toward those of different racial or ethnic heritages. Populist politicians often fan these sentiments to carry certain bloc votes. When residents bother to participate in county board meetings through interactive cable, the exchange frequently becomes acrimonious, and the audio is deleted. A few meetings have ended abruptly when opponents on the losing side of an issue found ways to disable the system. Public hearings are becoming few.

The primary ticket to middle-class income is entrepreneurial skill and luck. The county is filled with small businesses, many located in homes. The competition is fierce, most businesses are undercapitalized, and few fulfill the entrepreneur's hopes. Bankruptcy rates are high as there is little accumulated capital to finance business ventures. Private school enterprises are one of the few local growth industries. With the desire to control children's education coupled with inadequate public school financing, high student–teacher ratios, and electronic education, many parents scrape together tuition. Employment is high, though the lower paying jobs of the service and hospitality industries dominate. The majority of residents are divided between the working near poor, living in deteriorating neighborhoods but who still see themselves as middle class, and a semipermanent underclass living in ghetto-type neighborhoods whose gangs, crime, and drug use leave people feeling they live in a combat zone. The limited public transportation stops at the borders of these areas. The rich live in walled communities and high rises with maximum security protection, referred to by the local media as "Fortress Arlington." Although vigilantism is not formally structured, people believe strongly that families should take care of their own and friends should come to the aid of friends. Law-enforcement officials have written off parts of Arlington as impossible to police.

New technology is inexpensive and widespread. Advanced personal computer/entertainment systems have replaced television and provide the focal point of quality family time. Despite the importance of family and friends to survival, divorce and family dysfunction have not decreased. Electronics provide access to information and the link to those outside an individual's local group who hold the same political beliefs. Thus, censorship groups, gun-control advocates, and militia activists stay in touch across the country.

Greatly reduced because of budget cuts, the library is no longer a very important service of local government. Security and heavily used, poorly maintained buildings are administrative concerns. Through technological advances the library is accessible electronically from home and remains one way in which people can try to "pull themselves up by their bootstraps."

6

Student Technology Fee
A Case Study at the University of Nebraska–Lincoln

JIM EMAL
COMPUTING COORDINATOR FOR IANR COMMUNICATIONS &
INFORMATION TECHNOLOGY, UNIVERSITY OF NEBRASKA–LINCOLN

JOAN GIESECKE
DEAN OF LIBRARIES,
UNIVERSITY OF NEBRASKA–LINCOLN

All organizations have developed processes they use to make strategic decisions. These processes often follow an internal logic of how the external environment functions. That logic may or may not reflect the actual environment in which the organization exists. If the internal logic of the organization meshes well with the environment, the organization is likely to flourish. If it does not, the organization can find itself in the proverbial backwater, disenfranchised from its customers and failing to succeed in a changing environment.

How can managers help their organizations examine their internal processes and test their version of reality? One planning tool that can help free the organizational decision-making processes from stagnation is scenario planning. Using a simpler model of scenario planning than the process that is often used for organizational-wide planning and focusing on a specific decision question can help managers design better strategies and make better decisions for their organizations. At the University of Nebraska–Lincoln (UNL), the Information Services Unit used scenario planning techniques as part of an overall effort to establish a student technology fee to provide ongoing computer support for students. This case study outlines how UNL was able to use the scenario planning technique to move beyond traditional planning efforts and develop more-creative solutions for the problems of providing computer support on campus.

Background

As is true at most universities today, UNL faced the problem of increasing demand for computer support services by students in a time of decreasing support from the state for the university. In 1994 an external review team assessing computer support on campus concluded that the university needed to create an ongoing funding process for computer support and for expanded services for students. Attempts to obtain additional funding from the legislature or from the university were unsuccessful. By 1996 the "support crisis" was becoming critical and the associate vice chancellor for information services (IS) determined that something different had to be done if the computing area were to provide even basic services to students. The idea of charging a student fee was proposed internally within IS and was discussed as one way to obtain ongoing funding. The IS computing managers met in the summer of 1996 to brainstorm how a student fee might be used. The list of services generated by this internal group was very basic and concentrated on upgrading current hardware and software. Included in the list were also wish-list-type items: expenditure on infrastructure, networking, and cutting-edge technologies that could not be funded with current dollars. The justification for using student fees for infrastructure centered on computing needs as a whole and did not focus very directly on student interests. In all, the list was not very innovative, reflected the personal concern of the managers, and did not look at how students might react to the fee proposal.

In June 1996 the associate vice chancellor for IS concluded that the group needed to have a more-imaginative, innovative proposal if it were to capture the imagination of the chancellor, vice chancellors, deans, faculty, and students. The proposal had to appeal to and have the support of the students to be accepted by the administration and by the board of regents.

The associate vice chancellor for IS suggested scenario planning as the tool to use to help the managers move beyond their own views of reality and of the future to develop a more forward-thinking proposal. It was felt that scenario planning would help the group explore a wide range of possible futures to aid the UNL leadership's decision-making process.

Process

Starting a new approach to attack an existing problem required some study. The scenario planning process was a new experience for the planning team leadership as well as for most of the team membership. Therefore, a brief time was expended learning about scenario theory. The team leaders referred chiefly to Peter Schwartz's *The Art of the Long View* and to his site on the World Wide Web at http://www.gnb.com.[1] Additional readings were obtained from following links at this site.

Essentially, the team leadership became comfortable with the scenario planning process and optimistic about the potential for success, but the leaders never became experts or gurus on the subject. It's important to note that the scenario planning process can be effectively employed without credentialed leadership in the theory or practice. As noted by David Mercer, a simpler process for scenario planning can be effective in handling uncertainty. The greatest value of the process is that it helps managers broaden their viewpoints and extend their planning horizons.[2] A practical, simpler approach is particularly effective in addressing issues that are narrower than planning the overall strategic agenda for an organization.

A scenario planning team of fifteen persons was assembled. The majority of team membership came from within the department of information services, a large educational support unit that includes libraries, telecommunications, and computer services. Student representatives were from the senate computational services committee and university library student employee pool. The chair of the faculty teaching and learning technology roundtable contributed a teaching perspective to the team.

It is important to note here that the planning team represented the key groups that would be affected by a student technology fee and included representatives that were most likely to be directly involved in the services that a fee would support. By involving in the planning process those closest to the problems of student access to technology, the managers felt they would benefit from a fresh perspective on the issue and could begin to identify problems that would arise in trying to implement yet another fee for students. The planning group was provided with reading materials on the use of scenario planning, provided examples from the literature of successful teamwork tasks in this area, and given the opportunity to develop a supportable list of benefits resulting from a student technology fee at UNL.

Given the narrow focus of the problem facing the planning team, the team chose to follow Mercer's simpler process for developing mini-scenarios rather than using the full scenario planning process as outlined in chapter 1. Mercer uses six steps to create a more-focused scenario planning process:

1. Identifying drivers for change
2. Linking the key factor
3. Producing the initial mini-scenarios
4. Reducing the number of scenarios
5. Writing the scenarios
6. Identifying issues that arise[3]

Identifying the Drivers for Change

Two meetings of the team were planned. Much of the first meeting was dedicated to the process—learning about scenario planning, reviewing the team charge, and listening to assumptions on the subject at hand. This session concluded with a period of unrestricted brainstorming on the environment for technology and on the factors that were likely to have an impact on student use of technology on campus. A faculty colleague, experienced with the scenario planning process, opened the meeting with an overview of his experiences and provided valuable assurance that positive results were possible from this investment in energies and resources.

The group then broke into two subgroups to identify factors in the environment that would have an impact on student use of technology. These brainstorming sessions resulted in two extensive lists of more than thirty elements. The elements ranged from the mundane, such as a need for an easier way to obtain a parking permit, to the more controversial, such as how to upgrade faculty skills to meet growing student expectations about the use of technology. The planning group then adjourned for one week to give the team leaders an opportunity to consolidate the information from the first session and to provide participants with feedback for the second session.

Linking the Key Factors

In the week between the two planning sessions, team leaders met to decipher notes from the brainstorming sessions and to set the stage for the first attempts at scenario creation. They consolidated and reviewed the brainstorming lists. This smaller group of four managers used the lists to identify two factors considered most important and most uncertain: the skill level of students entering the university and the types of services students would want to support. The consensus of the steering committee was that these two factors provided a broad enough framework to consider the issues under discussion. (See figure 6.1.)

Figure 6.1 UNL Matrix of Uses of Technology to Enhance Student Learning

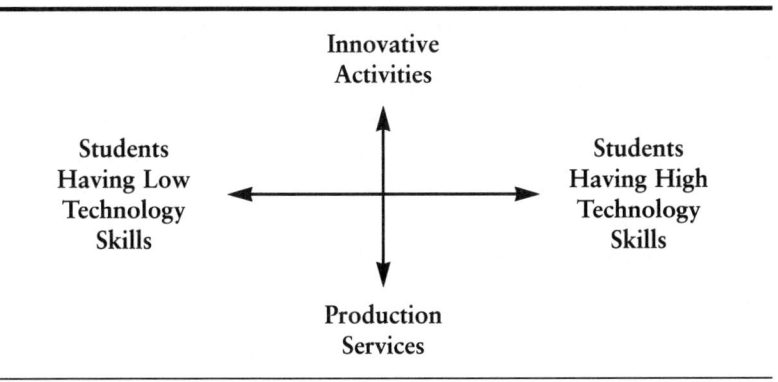

```
                    Innovative
                    Activities
                        ↑
  Students              │              Students
  Having Low    ←───────┼───────→     Having High
  Technology            │              Technology
  Skills                │              Skills
                        ↓
                    Production
                    Services
```

The factors were listed on a continuum to form the basis for scenario development. Skill level was measured on a continuum from low-skill students with little or no experience with or exposure to computers to high-skill students who own their own computers. *Students having low technological skill* do not generally rely on it and are uncertain about its value. *Students having high technological skill* are very dependent on it, demanding to use it at all times and in all places possible. Services were described on a continuum from innovative, cutting-edge services and technology to production-oriented, basic services. *Innovative activities* would be experimental activities based on emerging, "bleeding edge"technologies, for example, a metropolitan area wireless data network. *Production services* would be reliable services based on current, proven technologies, for example, current Ethernet networks. The matrix from these two factors described four possible scenario stories: high-skill students interested in cutting-edge services; high-skill students interested in production services; low-skill students curious about cutting-edge technology; and low-skill students seeking basic, efficient services.

Although usually the whole planning group would be involved in choosing the factors that frame the scenario development, the team leaders decided that in the interest of time they would complete this step themselves. However, the team leaders were careful to be sure that the major issues identified by participants were covered in the matrix design.

Producing the Initial Mini-Scenario Elements

The second planning session, held one week later, started with a brief recap of session one and a description of the scenario matrix structure and its use. The group then divided into two subgroups to generate the key elements they believed should be a part of each of the four possible scenarios. Next, the groups came together to share these lists and decide on the common elements to be included in each scenario. The group concluded with the creation of a recommended list of possible expenditures to be made with funds generated from new student-technology fees based on the elements of the scenarios.

Reducing the Number of Scenarios to Two or Three

The team leaders met again after the planning session to consolidate the input and to look for common elements that would allow the team to develop two scenarios from the planning process. The group chose to divide the scenarios based on student skill level, outlining a scenario for low-skill students and one for high-skill students. The team leaders wanted to be sure that the scenarios focused on student needs and not on technology so that the students would be able to see what benefits they might get from a student technology fee.

Writing the Scenarios

One member of the team then volunteered to draft an initial story for each of the scenarios, incorporating the elements outlined by the planning group. The stories were written from the student viewpoint, focusing on how a student might use technology on campus once the fee was in place and new equipment and services were available. Each story started with two new students beginning classes in the fall semester and discussed how the students would encounter and use technology in their first few weeks at the university. The low-skill students were described as inexperienced but curious about technology, a bit afraid of using the various computer services, and in need of supportive training programs. The high-skill students were viewed as having high expectations of the type of technology they would find on campus and as wanting to immediately "plug into" the technology system. Using the simpler scenario planning process, only two scenarios were developed to describe the students' skill levels. (See figure 6.2. Also see the appendix to this chapter for the complete stories.)

The draft stories were shared among the team leaders, edited, and polished for sharing with the planning group.

Identifying Issues That Arise

The final step in the scenario process was to develop strategies that would be most likely to succeed if either of the scenarios proved to

The Application

Figure 6.2 UNL Student Technology Fee Scenario Matrix

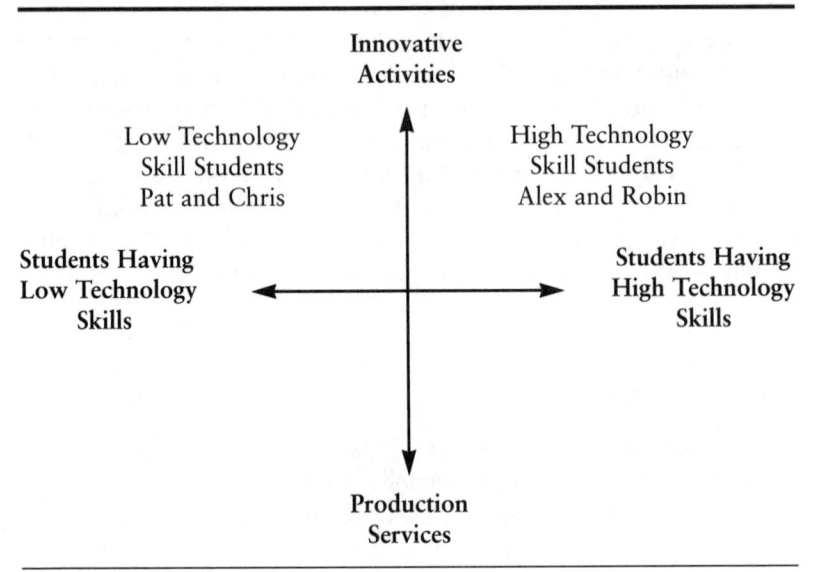

```
                        Innovative
                        Activities
                            ▲
        Low Technology     │     High Technology
        Skill Students     │     Skill Students
        Pat and Chris      │     Alex and Robin
Students Having            │            Students Having
Low Technology    ◄────────┼────────►   High Technology
Skills                     │            Skills
                           │
                           │
                           ▼
                        Production
                        Services
```

be an apt description of the student expectations for technology. To determine what could actually be done, the team leaders took the list of possible items or activities to fund with a technology fee as developed in the various planning group sessions and mapped the list to the four quadrants of the matrix. Those items that fit three or four of the quadrants were then examined to see if they appeared to be good purchases from the technology fee. For example, increasing student access to computers and upgrading computer equipment in the public labs was seen as benefiting students with low skills needing both production services and some innovative technology and high-skill students seeking production services. High-skill students seeking advanced, cutting-edge equipment would need a more-specialized lab area. Creating a student-centered learning space by placing a computer lab in the libraries and incorporating it into the regular electronic library services was also seen as benefiting most of the student groups. Adding a text and technology area to the library lab would make the space more useful to high-skill, innovative students. (See figure 6.3.)

Figure 6.3 Possible Uses for the UNL Technology Fee

Strategies	High Skill/ Production	High Skill/ Innovative	Low Skill/ Innovative	Low Skill/ Production
Develop student peer mentoring	X	X		X
Improve network	X	X		X
Increase student access to equipment and student labs	X	X		X
Provide opportunity for students to teach in classroom	X			
Support faculty development	X	X	X	X
Create multimedia center for students	X	X		
Survey/visit peer institutions	X			
Create student-centered learning space and environment (in libraries)	X	X	X	X
Provide greater access to existing electronic resources	X			
Provide more electronic resources	X	X		
Develop easy interfaces	X		X	X
Create Internet courses		X		
Provide access to experts		X		
Provide internships (work with faculty)		X		
Increase data storage space		X		
Promote technology literacy (graduate and undergraduate)			X	X
Disseminate information about services			X	X
Integrate technology into university business functions			X	X
Develop strategic flexibility			X	
Upgrade supported classrooms				X
Provide multimedia classroom orientation				X

Research and Benefit Assessment

Another important task for the team leadership was to review other Big 12 university policies in this area of student fee assessment and come up with plausible proposals for UNL administrators. All but two other Big 12 universities had already implemented some type of student technology support fee. Team leaders then gathered appropriate information regarding the total number of credit hours taken at UNL each year and estimated what the potential income to a support fund would be within a range of fee assessment levels. For each $1 per credit hour assessment, the fund would realize approximately $600,000 in income. Eventually a final assessment figure of $5 per credit hour, phased in over a three-year period, was agreed upon and proposed to the administration.

Student Support

Following the scenario planning team meetings, a brief white paper incorporating the two scenarios was prepared that identified the goals and outlined major benefits of a technology fee. The white paper was shared with various administrators, advisory groups, and deans. Reactions from these administrative groups were used to refine the proposal before sharing it with key student leadership.

Arrangements were made for the team leadership to meet with representative groups of university students, share the information from the scenario planning process and the white paper, and record student reactions and recommendations. Seven sessions were arranged and held on both UNL campuses, involving a variety of students, many representing larger student groups, such as the Student Senate, Greek Affairs, and Residence Halls Association. Detailed notes were taken from these informal group discussions, and a summary was prepared for comparison with the original needs list developed via the scenario planning team approach. Most major ideas paralleled each other, that is, requests for newer computer lab hardware, extended hours in the public computer labs, more and better prepared lab consultants, and better access to the World Wide Web. Ideas unique to the student groups also surfaced quickly. An excellent example was a request for child day-care services at one or more of the computer lab sites. The students pointed out that UNL provided routine day-care services in the recreation department so parents could participate in these activities while their children were supervised but provided no such services so parents could study, attend classes, or work in the public computer classrooms.

Acting on Students' Input and Administrative Promises

Success stories result from successful actions. All the work and effort put forth into the process of identifying student and classroom technology needs, delineating wish lists, and suggesting economically sound solutions would be fruitless without a concluding *action step*. The scenario plans offered views of the possible futures, but it was up to the IS and university leadership to construct the pathways to those futures. In rapid succession, while students were still on campus in the spring of 1997, the UNL chancellor and the associate vice chancellor for IS took the proposal for a phased-in student technology fee to the deans, to the administration, and then to the university board of regents and the president's office. Five student leaders accompanied the team to the regents' meeting where formal approval was obtained. Student input and support during the scenario planning process and the subsequent student discussion sessions resulted in a very positive reception of the idea, enactment of the credit-hour assessment charges, and the prioritizing of technology fund expenditures. More than 200 new computer stations were in place by the fall semester, computer labs were staffed for extended hours, a lab was opened in the main library, and more help would become available to students via a proposed new student-technology help desk program.

Assessment

Could the IS unit have successfully implemented a student technology fee without using the scenario planning process? One could say that a fee was inevitable and would have been implemented eventually. However, it may well have taken more than six months to accomplish the goal, delaying the improvement of computer services to students by at least a year or more.

Why was the scenario planning successful? Scenario development helped refocus the managers' efforts from solving the student-support problem using old mental models to looking at how the environment was changing, listening to what students felt they would need, and examining more than one solution or possible future for student support. By examining multiple futures and alternatives, the group was able to design strategies to meet a broad spectrum of needs. The process also gave the managers valuable insights into their customers' needs and views on current services. The scenarios helped managers determine which strategies were most likely to appeal to a broad base of students. They also saw how to target some strategies to smaller, more-specialized constituencies. For example, adding authoring software to a lab and creating a development center for students interested in producing their own CD-ROM products will appeal to a small group of students. This strategy was quite popular with some members of the IS unit and was given a high priority by some managers. However, after the scenario planning process, this strategy was seen as a lower priority to be addressed after more-basic student needs such as extended hours for labs could be met.

One lesson that was clear from this process and that helped managers see long-range possibilities as well as near-term needs was that exploring possible futures provides more flexibility for managers in changing environments than trying to guess and develop a preferable future. Through scenario planning, the group will be able to build multiple paths to the future by putting one brick in place at a time.

Notes

1. Peter Schwartz, *The Art of the Long View: Planning For the Future in an Uncertain World* (New York: Currency Doubleday, 1991).
2. David Mercer, "Simpler Scenarios," *Management Decisions* 3 (July 1995): 33.
3. Mercer, "Simpler Scenarios."

APPENDIX

UNL Student Technology Fee Scenarios

High Technology Skill

Students Alex and Robin come to UNL with a laptop computer or a PC and assume that they will be able to plug in their equipment as they unpack and settle into the dorms. Alex and Robin already have an Internet Service Provider (ISP), but they expect to be able to quickly add a UNL e-mail account. Alex and Robin regularly surf the Net; read electronic journals; play games; and chat with friends, classmates, and cyber friends from all over. They are already familiar with the UNL home page, the library catalog, etc. They wonder what else is available to the campus students.

Alex and Robin expect to conduct university business by computer. They feel that they should be able to update address lists or establish a borrowers record with the library, for example, from the dorm room.

Alex and Robin explore the campus and find that one of their classes is in a high-tech classroom where the professor will be able to use multimedia; another class is in a space with a computer workstation for each student. They are excited that technology will be used in the teaching process.

Alex and Robin want to learn more about how instructional technology can help them in their course work. They find the student information and instruction center, a learning space in the new addition to the library with its state-of-the-art and leading-edge computers or "scholars' workstations." From these workstations, they can use a variety of networked information resources available from the libraries and other sources, consult encyclopedias and other reference tools, use course reserve material, and access Internet sites. The user interface looks familiar, is easy to understand, and allows them to move easily among a wide variety of electronic resources. They can then access software needed to put a paper together or create a presentation. When they have a question, they can consult with faculty, computer experts, and library experts who provide guidance as well as teaching them how to solve their own problems. But mostly, they are happy to be left alone to explore and discover.

Alex and Robin are pleased to see that the learning space includes a group setting, where they can work with classmates on a project, as well as individual study spaces.

Alex and Robin want to do more. They want to create their own multimedia products and to try out leading-edge technology to see how that technology can help them in their classwork. They find the new media center for students. Here is an experimental lab where they can be creative, create new products, and explore ideas. They find they spend as much time helping others as they spend learning about the technologies themselves.

As Alex and Robin take more classes, their interest in helping others grows. They sign up to be student mentors, working with other students to use instructional technology and information resources. Alex and Robin are getting paid to do what they enjoy best—learning how to take advantage of technology to advance their learning process while helping their friends and colleagues learn to use these tools.

Alex and Robin also find opportunities to work with faculty in developing multimedia presentations and resources. As part of an internship, Alex and Robin assist a favorite professor, who has a semester study leave, develop a new course that will be delivered both on campus and to distance-education students.

Low Technology Skill

Students Pat and Chris are nervous. They just completed new-student enrollment and are bewildered by the size and complexity of the university. Although Pat and Chris did great in high school, their school had few computers, and the two students are only vaguely aware of the world of the Internet. Pat and Chris are most concerned with finding the right classroom. Signing up for an e-mail account and using a busy public lab is more than they want to tackle right now.

Pat and Chris discover that one of their classes is taught in a high-technology, multimedia classroom. The professor plans to use e-mail to distribute information about the class to the students. Everyone is expected to participate in these e-mail conversations. Pat and Chris are thinking of dropping this course.

Pat and Chris's resident advisor steps in to help. The RA is well versed in the intricacies of getting an e-mail account and signing up to use the system. The RA invites a training student/mentor to a dorm program to help show their floor how to use the UNL system.

The student/mentor explains e-mail accounts, provides basic information about the library system, and shows the group how to get onto the Internet. The relaxed, informal atmosphere of the dorm floor sets the tone for the presentation. Pat and Chris see some hope that they might survive the technology.

Pat and Chris visit the student information and instruction center as part of their classwork that requires use of library resources. Here Pat and Chris find computers and helpful consultants to gain access to the library information system. The interface is easy to use, and staff are available to answer their questions. More importantly, the other students in the area are willing to help, too. Pat and Chris are glad to find they can get to course reserves and complete assignments that are due.

Pat and Chris also find the public labs on campus. Here they can access e-mail, use word processing, access the libraries' catalog, and print term papers that are due. They are relieved to find that the interface is easy to use and that the menus make sense to those with little or no computer vocabulary.

By the end of the semester, Pat and Chris are ready to think about getting a computer for their dorm room. They consult with the computer shop where they get advice on options that they can purchase and rent a computer to see if they really like it.

Pat and Chris are slowly beginning to feel comfortable with instructional technology. Although they rely on others in their class groups to construct PowerPoint presentations, they are comfortable enough to participate in planning these presentations.

Pat and Chris are also comfortable enough to use the network system to register for classes, request a book from the library, and get a parking permit. They are glad that they no longer have to stand in long lines but are also glad they didn't have to work with the system as new students.

Pat and Chris realize that some professors are not very comfortable with the technology. They see them also struggling to learn how to use all the new systems. Although Pat and Chris hope the professors figure this all out someday, they are not too terribly concerned. The longer it takes the professors to learn the technology, the more time Pat and Chris have to figure it out too.

Pat and Chris's skill levels may seem basic, but they have advanced to the point where they can cope with the changing technology and rely on fellow students, staff, librarians, RAs, etc., to help them face each new challenge.

7

Preparing Librarians for the Twenty-First Century
Scenarios for the Future

NANCY BUSCH
DEPUTY DIRECTOR
NEBRASKA LIBRARY COMMISSION, LINCOLN, NEBRASKA

The four scenarios in this chapter each tell a different story about how the role, education, and training of library and information professionals in Nebraska may change as we move into the twenty-first century. The scenarios are intended to provide a context for thinking about the changes taking place in the library and information field and in the education and training of the field's practitioners. They are not predictions; rather, they describe a range of plausible future outcomes that can be used to extend the boundaries within which library and information professionals think about the future as it might appear in the year 2007, less than a decade from now.

The focus of this scenario building exercise is public library and information practitioners in Nebraska. Although the continuing education needs for school library media specialists and academic and special librarians in Nebraska may be similar or overlapping, the driving forces for the sectors in which these practitioners operate are considered to be sufficiently different to preclude examination in this illustration. Key stakeholders in this environment are the Nebraska Library Commission, the regional library systems, public librarians, library board trustees, city councils, and the customers of Nebraska's public libraries.

The purpose of this scenario building exercise is to confront the questions:

> What are the critical skills Nebraska's public library and information practitioners will need in the twenty-first century?
>
> How should the Nebraska Library Commission be positioning itself to facilitate the education and training of public library and information professionals for the twenty-first century?
>
> Who are the key partners with which the Nebraska Library Commission should be collaborating to identify and deliver these skills?

To address these questions, we must also ponder the likely futures and uncertainties facing public libraries and the communities in which they exist because they form the basis for the practice of library and information professionals.

> What role will public libraries in Nebraska play in the twenty-first century?
>
> Will Nebraska's smaller communities remain viable?
>
> Will citizens continue to support public libraries in the twenty-first century?

Sources of input for the scenario building purpose were contained in a series of public forums and visioning sessions held throughout Nebraska during 1996 and 1997 under the theme of Libraries for the Twenty-First Century. Extracted from these planning sessions are comments and ideas relating to the education and training of library and information practitioners. Optimally, development of these scenarios would involve a group of individuals of the various key stakeholders brought together for the purpose of engaging in such a process. In this case, the brainstorming and identification of factors and driving trends has come out of a variety of recent dialogues in Nebraska on a broader range of topics relating to the library and information service needs of citizens in the twenty-first century.[1]

In addition, a recent report by the Benton Foundation on the public's opinion of library leaders' visions of the future provided grist for the mill in building these scenarios.[2] Based on research conducted in 1996 with public library leaders, public opinion surveys, and a focus group of sophisticated library users, the Benton Foundation report is a rich source of factors, trends, and speculations on library futures.

A key assumption is that the individual library and information practitioner is critical to the design and delivery of quality library and information services. As Alice Bryan pointed out some forty-five years ago in *The Public Librarian,* "The public library is no exception to the general rule that an institution is as good as its personnel. What public libraries in the United States accomplish from day to day depends largely upon the qualities, specialized skills, and working effectiveness of the people who operate them."[3]

Driving Forces

Although we cannot know specifically what the future will hold, we can see in the present a number of factors, trends, or driving forces that, if continued on their present course, may change the role and nature of library and information professionals during the next ten years.

In a recent *Library Journal* editorial, Anne Woodsworth, dean of the Palmer School of Library and Information Science, asserts new critical competencies for library and information professionals. As Woodsworth notes, change is running rampant in libraries, with technology as the driving force. When coupled with millennium fever, the result is constant questioning about our future and the competencies we will need to survive professionally.[4] Woodsworth's investigations lead her to believe that technological competencies are most essential for all librarians. Other competencies required include leadership, communication, evaluation, and teaching skills as well as the ability to develop new services, shape information policy, and lead discussions on the ethical use of information.

Toni Carbo, dean of the School of Information Sciences at the University of Pittsburgh, frames such competencies as mediacy skills that include the ability to

explore information space

discover and learn

find and retrieve information

evaluate, organize, manage, and preserve it
create, disseminate, and use it[5]

Added to this list is the need to understand ethical issues surrounding the generation and use of information and to form partnerships between information producers and users to develop mediacy skills.

Along these same lines, several graduate schools of library and information science are in the throes of curriculum reform that attempt to address the changing roles of those practicing the profession in diverse settings. The University of Michigan School of Information, for example, notes in various publications:

> Information professionals will play an increasingly vital role in empowering individuals, communities, and organizations to capture the promise of the information age. The School of Information embraces a vision that harmonizes people, information systems, and organizations to improve the quality of life. Our mission is to discover the principles and concepts that will enable society to realize this vision and to educate new generations of professionals who will put that vision into place.[6]

> [The information infrastructure of the twenty-first century] . . . requires professionals who have acquired knowledge and skills to provide the intellectual structures through which information is organized. It requires system architects who understand not only technology but the entire spectrum of social, economic, legal, and human factors involved. It requires those who possess the analytical capabilities to assure the quality of the information and the service orientation to enable those in the communities they serve to access the resources they need. They must have a deep commitment and knowledge to use the new digital technologies to reduce barriers of access for all, perhaps especially those now disadvantaged by geographical, educational, or economic barriers.[7]

Similarly, the Special Libraries Association and the Medical Library Association have put forth their visions of the requisite professional and personal competencies for library and information professionals, which mirror those identified by Woodsworth, Durrance, and others.

Nebraska, like most states in the Great Plains region, does not have a graduate school of library and information science. Nebraskans have had, in recent years, in-state access to a master's degree program in this field through the Emporia (Kansas) State University School of Library and Information Management Distance Program. However, without the continuous presence of such a program to offer professional development opportunities for library and information practitioners, the Nebraska Library Commission has become the de facto source of education and training, particularly for the public library sector. With a state population of approximately 1.6 million, Nebraska has 234 public libraries, 166 of which are accredited, meeting the minimal standards for receiving state aid. Ninety-three percent of these 234 public libraries are located in communities with populations of 10,000 or less. Thus, the majority of the public librarians in Nebraska are practicing in what many would consider rural environments.

When we say *librarian* in Nebraska, what do we mean in comparison with the competencies proposed above? Only sixteen public library directors in the state have a Master's Degree in Library and Information Science, whereas seventy-four public librarians who are nondirectors hold that degree. Those Nebraska public librarians with master's degrees are for the most part concentrated in the larger (over 10,000 population) communities, which leaves few if any master's degree directors in the under-10,000 population communities. This is well below the national percentage for rural public library directors that based on 1989 data, was nearly 21 percent with the graduate degree.[8]

Although data are not collected on the age and gender of Nebraska's public librarians, it may be safe to assume that nearly 90 percent are female and the average age is likely to be around 50. These figures would be consistent with national data on rural public librarians that were collected by the author in 1989. Staffing for the 218 public libraries located in communities of 10,000 or less totals 246 full-time equivalents, which translates into slightly more than one full-time staff member for each library. The average hourly salary of public library directors ranges from $5.51 in libraries in communities of 1,000 or fewer, of which there are 96 in Nebraska, to $33.58 in communities over 50,000, of which there are only two in Nebraska.[9]

In Nebraska's smaller communities, which again are in the majority, new library directors and other staff are most likely to be recruited from within a community and may not have had any prior experience or education relevant to the position. The educational requirements are lower in smaller public libraries than in those serving a larger population, and there is a general lack of understanding of the qualities and qualifications needed on the part of the library boards or local officials who recruit librarians. The public librarian certification process, offered through the Nebraska Library Commission, serves as the primary source of education and training for these librarians.

Begun in 1987, the public librarian certification program is designed to

- improve library service throughout the state
- motivate librarians to develop skills through basic and continuing education
- upgrade the image of libraries and librarians
- provide guidelines for public library boards to use in selecting and retaining personnel

The intent of this program is also to recognize public librarians who update their knowledge and skills on a continuing basis to provide better library service for the community. One of the requirements for certification specifies that librarians complete a series of four basic skills courses designed to focus on core library services and functions such as collection development, organization of materials, public services, and public library administration.

There is uncertainty as to the effectiveness of such programs in retooling library staff to develop the competencies and skills described earlier. The content of many of the educational offerings is based on traditional library science paradigms, and the basic skills and other continuing-education offerings have limited impact on meeting a large and diverse need. As Mary Bushing noted in her research on the professionalization of rural librarians,

> The autonomous and varied state programs for the education and training of rural public librarians appear to be uneven on a number of scales: quality of the educational content, quality of

the educational delivery, quality of the educators, frequency of delivery, responsiveness to the librarians, attitudes and friendliness of providers, program design, funding, and continuing consulting services. These vary greatly from state to state. National or multistate cooperation might be able to provide a better end product more efficiently. Graduate schools of library science, distance education technology, Internet conferencing capabilities, and appropriate program design can all contribute to the creation and delivery of quality basic continuing or preservice education to meet the needs of rural librarians across a range of political and geographic boundaries.[10]

Dimensions of Uncertainty

Developing descriptions of potential futures involves embracing uncertainties that may face communities and libraries as they move into the next century. There are many uncertainties concerning the future of public libraries in Nebraska. One involves the viability of many of the smaller communities in a predominantly rural state. Inasmuch as public libraries in Nebraska are created and primarily funded on the local level, libraries and communities are inextricably linked. A healthy, vital community is fundamental to create and support a healthy, vital public library. This dimension of community vitality, framed here as decline and renewal, creates one continuum of the matrix along which Nebraska communities and public libraries may be positioned in future scenarios.

Another key uncertainty, offered as a second dimension or continuum for the scenario matrix, is the degree to which communities and their public libraries are practicing autonomy or collaboration in their approaches to development. One could reason that communities or public libraries may be in the process of renewal but approach renewal or revitalization autonomously rather than working collaboratively with other communities or libraries within the region or state. These uncertainties are hypothesized to be the two key dimensions for construction of scenarios for future library and information service as they contribute to the overall, long-term viability of communities, hence their ability to support libraries.

102 *The Application*

Figure 7.1 Public Library Scenario Matrix

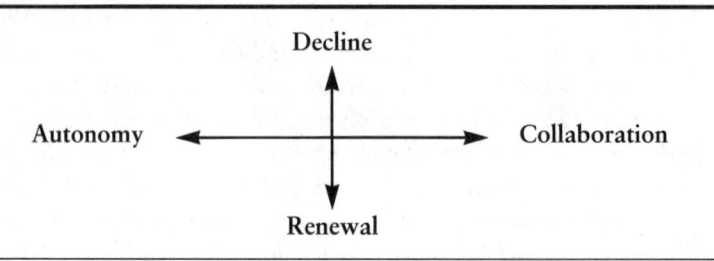

```
                    Decline
                      ▲
                      │
    Autonomy  ◄───────┼───────►  Collaboration
                      │
                      ▼
                    Renewal
```

These two axes then, decline vs. renewal and autonomy vs. collaboration, form the matrix on which four scenarios were developed. (See figure 7.1.)

Community/Library Scenario Matrix

Predetermined Elements

While these two axes help define and differentiate the four scenarios from one another, there are other issues and trends that will play a part in any scenario for the future of public libraries in Nebraska. The proliferation of information technology, personalization of information services, and increased competition for funding will be the three major elements considered as variables operating along with the dimensions of uncertainty, influencing each of the four scenarios in different ways.

PROLIFERATION OF INFORMATION TECHNOLOGY

Expanding use of information technology for Internet access, automation, community networking, distance learning, telecommuting, and creation of virtual workplaces is a well-documented force that is likely to continue. The speed at which information technology is diffusing into society in general and into public libraries in particular, is a matter of conjecture. The introduction of ever more-powerful telecommunications and computing technologies and the widening gap between citizens who can and cannot afford to own them are creating critical public policy and access issues. With an increasingly computer- and electronic information-literate public, the demand for more-sophisticated services has begun and will continue.

Information technology is enhancing public library and information service, but to what extent is such technology in place and used in Nebraska's public libraries? Can librarians keep pace with the education and training needed to successfully use such technology? Many Nebraska public libraries have automated and have access to the Internet through dial-up connections, with state and federal grants providing the hardware in many cases. The ability of staff in these libraries to continuously upgrade their systems, provide maintenance on the equipment, and access the training needed to optimize their use is limited, presenting a great challenge to providers of such education and training.

PERSONALIZATION OF INFORMATION SERVICES

Consider the following illustration from the education community:

> As a result of the convergence of computing, communications, and entertainment, the needs of the individual can be catered to with a degree of personalized precision undreamed of in the industrial era of mass production and mass markets. For the first time, it is possible to customize a range of experiences and products to suit one's special desires. People no longer watch the news, but turn to personalized electronic newspapers ("niche news") that speak to their specific concerns. They listen to business reports tailored to their individual portfolios. They shop for products at their favorite stores from huge online, interactive catalogues. They receive the training and education they want when and where they want it. Some companies market services which help individuals create the unique configurations that serve their needs. But more often, popularly available software and information services permit individuals to customize their own use of information. The individual reigns in the information kingdom. People participating in the new information economy come to expect highly individualized approaches to their needs. Just as broadcasting has been supplanted by narrowcasting and finally by direct interactive communications with "markets of one," so education has been transformed from the laying on of standardized lessons to a more Socratic drawing out . . . of each individual.[11]

This description is not of some faraway future but depicts reality for a small, but growing, population of techno-literate citizens who are increasingly reliant on instant access to customizable information. Findings in the Benton Foundation Report suggest that Americans who use computers at home are also public library users and support the idea of libraries investing in technology and digital information sources.[12] The jury is still out, however, on whether the younger generation (k–12) is likely to sustain such enthusiasm for the public library as an information provider.

In a recent issue of *Wired*, Brian Caulfield notes that with digital formats becoming the preferred way of storing and disseminating information, some librarians fear they could go the way of blacksmiths. Since 1976, 15 library schools have closed and the number of library school graduates has dropped from 8,037 in 1975–1976 to 4,845 in 1996.[13] Curricula in library schools that have survived tend to reflect an increased emphasis on the competencies and mediacy skills (described earlier by Woodsworth and Carbo).

Increased Competition for Funding

As competition increases for Nebraska's finite supply of tax revenues in upcoming years and as the state's population continues to shift, taxpayers and decision makers alike will need to become more involved and better educated about the fundamental issues facing the state as a whole.[14]

Public libraries and their communities face increased competition for funding on the local and state levels as we move into the twenty-first century. Property tax limitations and reform will require communities and libraries to search for alternative sources of revenue, such as sales tax, to support services. The position of public libraries among community priorities will become even more critical if libraries are to weather these shifts. The economic conditions for librarians operating these community libraries—salaries, benefits, staffing levels, continuing education opportunities, etc.—have never been adequate in Nebraska, so increased competition exacerbates the situation.

Nebraska's library and information practitioners will need to sharpen and apply their political and advocacy skills to successfully compete with other local and regional interests. Evidence of active partnerships or collaborations with other agencies and organizations will likely be one criterion for funding; another may be the willingness to serve a geographic area larger than a single community.

Four Scenario Narratives

> Perceiving alternative futures in the present requires a willing suspension of disbelief.... Scenarios provide stories which draw the listener into the narrative to help them think that the unthinkable may be quite plausible.... In this way, scenarios help us come to grips with what we feel, hope, expect, fear for the future.[15]

The following four scenarios were developed from the factors outlined in the development of the matrix. (See figure 7.2.)

Impending Obscurity (Autonomy and Decline)

The year is 2007. Scores of Nebraska communities did not fare well in the past two decades of competition for economic viability. At best, many small communities are in stasis; however, most are in slow decline. Property tax reforms initiated in the late 1990s place more and more restrictions on the level and use of local property tax funds. With resources on the local level increasingly scarce, public services such as police, fire, sanitation, and streets receive a higher priority than public libraries when funds are allocated. Fund-

Figure 7.2 Scenario Matrix for Libraries of the Future

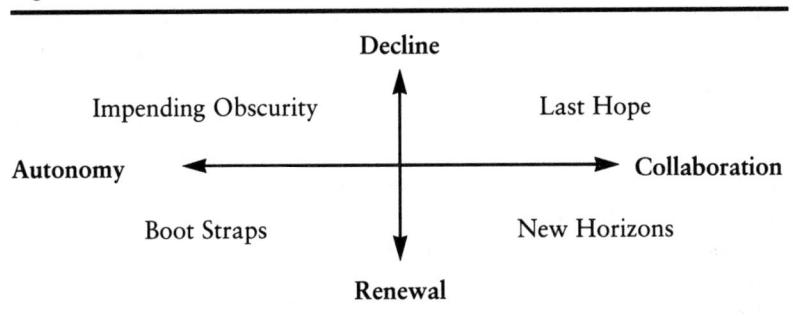

```
                       Decline
                         ↑
     Impending Obscurity │   Last Hope
                         │
Autonomy ◄───────────────┼───────────────► Collaboration
                         │
         Boot Straps     │   New Horizons
                         ↓
                       Renewal
```

ing of k–12 schools continues to consume a large portion of local and state tax dollars. Schools are well equipped with computing, telecommunications, and distance-learning capabilities, continuing to build on the infrastructure begun in the 1990s with state lottery and other special funding. Public libraries, on the other hand, have found it difficult to compete for state and local funds to update the information technology many of them put in place in the mid to late 1990s.

The community development and county extension professionals have taken over the major information-seeking, organizing, and dissemination roles in communities across Nebraska, and these services are being delivered and managed on a regional basis. New models for the design and delivery of community information services have emerged, fed by statewide initiatives from the School at the Center, the Rural Development Commission, the Nebraska Development Network, the State Department of Economic Development, and the University of Nebraska. Public librarians in most of the smaller communities are not key players in this information function since most librarians did not have the knowledge or political base to "sit at the table" with these other agencies and organizations when plans for community information service were being designed.

Libraries are still perceived as important public institutions, but by a dwindling number of citizens. Many libraries have been hard hit by local property tax limitations, closing down some libraries altogether and relegating other libraries to reading room status, with most books donated by community members. Libraries in the slightly larger communities are focused on more-traditional library services such as lending fiction, summer reading programs and story hours for children, and adult-oriented humanities programs. Nebraskans with more-sophisticated library and information needs travel to the larger libraries in their trade areas, coordinating their library use with other service needs such as shopping and visits to the doctor. Many pay handsome nonresident fees for the privilege.

Librarians in most communities are isolated from one another and have a tendency to be reactive rather than proactive in the design and delivery of services. Library staff are not involved in local community and economic development efforts, but they do attempt to survey their existing customers' needs from time to time. Salaries and benefits for library staff continue to be substandard, and the hours most libraries are open for service are few. Financial support for continuing education and training events is nonexistent, so librarians rarely have access to new knowledge and skills except those they are able to pick up on their own.

Last Hope (Collaboration and Decline)

The calendar reads 2007, and many Nebraska communities recognize that their efforts to attract new businesses and citizens to their towns have failed. Town leaders and citizens in smaller communities are realizing that their only hope for maintaining basic services in their locale is to join forces with other communities in their geographic area. Such alliances are proving to be one of the few sources of new funding and services for declining or static communities. Some counties have actually merged, pooling their resources in an attempt to stay afloat and support basic services such as road maintenance and emergency services. Others have banded together to share the cost of services, in many cases hiring circuit riders in various professions to deliver those services.

Nebraskans with the economic means have equipped their homes with the latest telecomputing systems and subscribe to a host of information resources through commercial companies. These techno-literate and connected Nebraskans are forming new virtual communities with like-minded others from all regions of the state and globe. For those who cannot afford the technology and information service subscriptions, the library is attempting to meet such needs, but with little success.

Libraries in these towns, especially those with populations of 2,500 or less, are poorly funded and staffed. Formation of library districts based on trade areas is also growing in popularity, with interlocal agreements becoming commonplace between two or more libraries. District governing councils or advisory groups are slowly replacing traditional library boards in individual communities. Towns without library facilities are being served by circuit librarians from larger communities who spend several hours each week with clients who have made arrangements for their services, which include consultation on specialized information needs and training on the use of online resources.

In some cases, public and school libraries have merged, enabling library staff to take full advantage of the advanced telecommunications and telecomputing infrastructure present in many of the schools. Some public librarians, having lower levels of education and skills than the school media specialists, have lost their positions in these mergers. Other public libraries are dealing with declining support by reducing print collections, offering dial-up access to catalogs and databases through larger libraries such as the Nebraska Library Commission and the University of Nebraska Libraries.

Public library staff in most communities are isolated from one another and from the education and training needed to keep pace with technological competencies and other skills deemed critical to the information profession. Some librarians are attempting to keep up with new skills and trends through basic skills classes and other workshops offered through the Nebraska Library Commission and the regional library systems. However, public library staff find it difficult to keep up with the skills needed to help citizens find their way through an increasingly complex and expensive information environment.

Boot Straps (Autonomy and Renewal)

By the year 2007 the economies in a majority of Nebraska's communities have improved, as locally based revitalization efforts have begun to bear fruit. Information technologies are becoming well-developed within renewal communities; however, there is limited cooperation and networking among communities in the region or state. To a certain extent, the information provision function is being met in many communities by a local consortium of economic developers, extension agents, and private-sector entrepreneurs. The focus of community development, although regional in intent, tends to meet with more success on the individual-community level, so few county- or region-wide consortia have materialized.

The public library's role is focused on providing programs and services on the local level and linking citizens who cannot afford the latest information technology. Librarians are becoming key players in Nebraska communities that have emerged successfully from two decades of competitive economic conditions. Due to their ability to contribute in positive, significant ways to economic development, librarians in these communities have positioned their libraries to serve as the centers for information technology and for the revitalization of civic life and lifelong learning.

With sufficient local funds for higher per-capita support for public library and information services, salaries and benefits for staff have improved in some communities, thus enabling them to recruit and retain library and information practitioners with higher levels of education, in some cases those with graduate degrees from library and information schools. Communities unable to afford such personnel have benefited from Library and Information Education Consortium's cyberworkshops, which help library practitioners keep pace with changing technologies and practices in the organization and dissemination of information.

New Horizons (Collaboration and Renewal)

The year is 2007. Community and economic development efforts, begun in the 1990s, contribute to population and economic growth patterns that are concentrated in the major trade and service areas of the state. In part, the community-renewal process has focused on successful integration into Nebraska communities of new citizens, some of whom have migrated into the state from other parts of the country, others from abroad. Statewide information technology planning and investments have resulted in a well developed and funded information infrastructure throughout the state. A variety of community services are being designed, funded, and delivered on a regional basis.

Property tax reform begun in the late 1990s, as well as efforts by the Nebraska Library Commission, the Nebraska Library Association, the Nebraska Unicameral legislature, and regional economic and community development organizations have been successful in helping create federated library districts. Formation of these taxing districts, of which there are twelve statewide, have provided sufficient, if not ample, local and state funding to achieve first-class library and information service for all Nebraskans. Computers and telecommunication technologies are common in public libraries throughout the state, with the districts playing a key role in the deployment of new technologies.

Librarians are viewed in their communities as key civic and information navigators, helping citizens, new and old alike, find their

110   The Application

way through a growing complex maze of government and privately produced information. Each library and information district has a hubquarters located in the region's major city, the natural location for major services such as health, trade, financial, and information services. The library hubquarters is staffed by several graduate-level library and information professionals who have aptitudes in a variety of areas, including the much-needed technological expertise for building and maintaining a complex, rich telecommunications infrastructure.

Local communities throughout the districts each have librarians called Community Information Specialists (CISs) who are part of the local community development team and who assist in the continuous assessment, design, and delivery of information services needed by local residents. These Community Information Specialists are employed by the district and work with other CISs throughout the district and state to create information systems that support the work of community developers and the general information needs of citizens.

Librarians are also instrumental in helping communities deal with social and political issues arising from renewal, such as increased ethnic diversity and new models of community based on larger, more-fluid populations. The knowledge and skills needed by these public library and information practitioners are offered through a consortium of providers, including the University of Nebraska, the Western Governor's University, educational service units, and graduate library and information science programs from around the country, and are delivered in a variety of means affordable and accessible to library staff statewide.

Implications and Strategies

> If you want a large number of people to work together in a coordinated way, they must share an image of the system of which they are a part.[16]

Looking at the four scenarios as a whole, what can be learned about the initial questions raised? Are there professional education and training strategies that, if initiated by the Nebraska Library Commission during the next few years, would help library and information practitioners function better in any of these possible futures? What elements or forces operating within these scenarios does the Library Commission have any ability to change or influence?

The four scenarios are best viewed as preliminary plots that need to be examined and further developed among the various key stakeholders in Nebraska. This scenario-building example demonstrates the complexities involved in a systemwide or statewide planning environment, with more forces operating in this milieu than in a single organization. Many more factors or driving trends, some of which cannot even be imagined at this point, will influence these scenarios in the future.

Accordingly, these futures or scenarios are even less predictable than ones that might be constructed for a single library or community. In scenario planning, no one scenario is more likely than any other to come to pass, nor is any scenario necessarily preferable to another (although the author may have a bias toward one or the other).

Developing scenarios or plots such as these will help Library Commission staff and other key stakeholders stay nimble as we move into the twenty-first century and will assist the Nebraska library community in gaining a better understanding of the competencies and roles they and their libraries may embody in the future. The challenge now is to take these scenarios and devise specific, yet flexible, strategies related to each of the futures. The Nebraska Library Commission may then make strategic decisions and allocate resources to support programs that seem compatible with evolution in each of the scenarios. The following strategies are offered as possibilities to initiate a dialogue:

> Form a federation of organizations sharing a common interest in the future of library education and training, including groups such as the Nebraska Library Association, the Nebraska Library Commission, library trustees, city and county officials, educators, library systems, graduate schools of library and information science, and citizen groups, to name a few.
>
> Adopt a set of principles relating to the education and training of library and information professionals that could be held up as a unifying force for future action. These principles might

include those competencies, skills, or knowledge bases upon which the stakeholders agree.

Develop specific strategies, actions, programs, and services that would achieve and sustain the levels of professional education and training needed by Nebraska's library and information personnel.

Identify unique roles for each of the federation members or partners to play in working toward commonly agreed-upon goals or principles.

Cultivate new models for the delivery of education and training modules that meet the varied and rapidly changing needs of library and information practitioners.

Monitor and evaluate progress being made toward achievement of the desired library and information educational levels and outcomes.

At the very time that citizens are wanting to use a greater range of information and have the expertise and technology to access it, library schools are closing and the number of graduates from those schools has been declining. States like Nebraska, without library schools, may find it more difficult to attract and keep library and information professionals. On the local level, most rural communities have never experienced the knowledge and skills that professionally educated and trained staff can bring to the table. This is a critical time for the library community, government officials, and citizens in Nebraska to envision and create a structure for professional development that will help transform library practitioners into the information specialists and navigators required for the next century.

Notes

1. "Visioning Sessions Generate Ideas," in Nebraska Library Commission home page; available from http://www.nlc.state.ne.us/about.html.
2. *Buildings, Books, and Bytes: Libraries and Communities in the Digital Age* (Washington, D.C.: Benton Foundation, 1996).
3. Alice I. Bryan, *The Public Librarian* (New York: Columbia Univ. Pr., 1952), 3.

4. Anne Woodsworth, "The Dean's List: New Library Competencies," *Library Journal* (15 May 1997): 46.
5. Toni Carbo, "Just-for-You Services on the Information Highway," *Information Standards Quarterly* 92 (Apr. 1997): 46.
6. Joan C. Durrance, "Reinventing the Community Information Professional: Strategies and Approaches Used to Develop Community Networking Knowledge" (cited 9 May 1997); available from http://www.si.unich.edu/Community/aliseCN_paper/aliseCN.html.
7. Faculty of the School of Information and Library Studies at the University of Michigan, "Educating Human Resources for the Information and Library Professions of the 21st Century" (19 May 1997), 3; available from http://www.si.unich.edu/cristaled/Kelloggproposal.html.
8. Nancy J. Busch, "Factors Relating to the Recuitment and Retention of Library Directors in Rural Libraries in the United States" (Ph.D. diss., University of Michigan, 1990), 119.
9. Nebraska Public Library Profile 1994–1995, Statistical Data. Lincoln: Nebraska Library Commission, November 1996.
10. Mary Catherine Bushing, "The Professionalization of Rural Libraries: Role Modeling, Networking and Continuing Education" (Ph.D. diss., Montana State University, 1995), 175–6.
11. Jay Ogilvy, "Education and Community: Four Scenarios for the Future of Public Education," in GBN Publication 2; available from http://www.gbn.org/Scenarios/NEA/Scenarios.html.
12. *Buildings, Books, and Bytes*, 17.
13. Brian Caulfield, "Morphing the Librarians: Fighting off Extinction in the Information Age," *Wired* 5, no. 8 (Aug. 1997): 64.
14. Steve Molnar, *The High Cost of Maintaining Ghost Town Government in Nebraska: State and Local Government in Nebraska*, Part II (Lincoln, Nebr.: Nebraska Tax Research Council, Apr. 1997), ii.
15. Peter Schwartz, *The Art of the Long View: Planning for the Future in an Uncertain World* (New York: Currency Doubleday, 1991), 2.
16. Karl-Henrik Robert, *The Natural Step: A Framework for Achieving Sustainability in Our Organizations* (Cambridge, Mass.: Pegasus Communications, 1997), 1.

Suggested Readings

Amara, R. "Views on Futures Research Methodology." *Futures* 23 (July/Aug. 1991): 645–9.

Ashley, W. C., and J. L. Morrison. *Anticipatory Management: 10 Power Tools for Achieving Excellence into the 21st Century.* Leesburg, Va.: Issue Action Publications, 1995.

Bishop, P., and J. W. King. "Vision Driven Change in Higher Education: A National Visioning Project." Paper presented at the World Future Society Meeting, Washington, D.C., July 17, 1996.

Buildings, Books, and Bytes: Libraries and Communities in the Digital Age. Washington, D.C.: Benton Foundation, 1996.

Busch, N. J. "Factors Relating to the Recruitment and Retention of Library Directors in Rural Public Libraries in the United States. Ph.D. diss., University of Michigan, 1990.

Bushing, M. C. "The Professionalization of Rural Librarians: Role Modeling, Networking and Continuing Education." Ph.D. diss., Montana State University–Bozeman, April 1995.

Clemons, E. K. "Using Scenario Analysis to Manage the Strategic Risks of Reengineering," *Sloan Management Review* 36, no. 4 (1995): 61–71.

de Geus, A. P. "Planning as Learning," *Harvard Business Review* 66, no. 2 (1988): 70–4.

Suggested Readings

Duncan, N. E., and P. Wack. "Scenarios Designed to Improve Decision Making," *Planning Review* 22, no. 2 (1994): 18–25, 46.

Durrance, J. "Reinventing the Community Information Professional: Strategies and Approaches Used to Develop Community Networking Knowledge." Available at http://www.si.umich.edu/Community/aliseCN_paper/aliseCN.html. (19 May 1997).

Elkington, J., and A. Trisoglio. "Developing Realistic Scenarios for the Environment: Lessons from Brent Spar." *Long Range Planning* 29, no. 6 (1996): 762–9.

Godet, M. "Integration of Scenarios and Strategic Management." *Futures* 20 (Sept. 1990): 730–9.

Kahn, H., and A. J. Wiener. *The Year 2000*. New York: Macmillan, 1967.

Mason, D. H. "Scenario-Based Planning: Decision Model for the Learning Organization." *Planning Review* 22, no. 2 (1994): 6–11.

May, G. H. *The Future Is Ours: Foreseeing, Managing and Creating the Future*. Westport, Conn.: Praeger, 1996.

Medical Library Association. *Platform for Change: The Educational Policy Statement of the Medical Library Association*. Chicago: MLA, 1996.

Morrison, J. L. "Scanning." In *Encyclopedia of the Future*, edited by G. T. Kurian and T. T. T. Molitor, 814–16. New York: Macmillan, 1996.

Morrison, J. L., and I. Wilson. "Analyzing Environments and Developing Scenarios for Uncertain Times." In *Planning and Management for a Changing Environment: A Handbook on Redesigning Postsecondary Institutions*, edited by Marvin Peterson, David Dill, and Lisa Mets. San Francisco: Jossey-Bass, forthcoming.

Nanus, B. "QUEST—Quick Environmental Scanning Technique." *Long Range Planning* 15, no. 2 (1982): 39–42.

Ogilvy, P. "Futures Studies and the Human Sciences: The Case for Normative Scenarios." In *New Thinking for a New Millenium*, edited by R. A. Slaughter, 26–83. New York: Routledge, 1996.

Renfro, W. L., and J. L. Morrison. "The Scanning Process: Getting Started." In *Applying Methods and Techniques of Futures Research: New Directions for Institutional Research*, no. 39, edited by J. L. Morrison, W. L. Renfro, and W. I. Boucher, 5–20. San Francisco: Jossey-Bass, 1983.

Schoemaker, P. J. H., and C. A. J. M. van der Heijden. "Integrating Scenarios into Strategic Planning at Royal Dutch/Shell." *Planning Review* 20, no. 3 (1992): 41–6.

Schwartz, P. *The Art of the Long View: Planning for the Future in an Uncertain World.* New York: Currency Doubleday, 1991.

———. "Composing a Plot for Your Scenario." *Planning Review* 20, no. 3 (1992): 4–8, 46.

———. "Scenarios," In *Encyclopedia of the Future*, edited by G. T. Kurian and T. T. T. Molitor, 816–17. New York: Macmillan, 1996.

Senge, P. M. and others. *The Fifth Discipline.* New York: Currency Doubleday, 1990.

———. *The Fifth Discipline Fieldbook: Strategies and Tools for Building a Learning Organization.* New York: Currency Doubleday, 1994.

Special Committee on Competencies for Special Librarians (Joanne Marshall, chair; Bill Fisher, Lynda Moulton, and Roberta Piccoli). "Competencies for Special Librarians for the 21st Century." Available at http://www.sla.org/professional/comp.html (3 June 1997).

Sunter, C. *Scenario Thinking: Pathways to the Future.* Washington, D.C.: TriMark Media, 1994. Video.

van der Heijden, K. *Scenarios: The Art of Strategic Conversion.* New York: Wiley, 1996.

Wack, P. "Scenarios: Shooting the Rapids." *Harvard Business Review* 63, no. 6 (1985): 139–50.

———. "Scenarios: Uncharted Waters Ahead." *Harvard Business Review* 63, no. 5 (1985): 73–89.

Wheatley, M. J. *Leadership and the New Science: Learning about Organization from an Orderly Universe.* San Francisco: Berrett-Koehler, 1994.

Wheatley, M. J., and M. Kellner-Rogers. *A Simpler Way.* San Francisco: Berrett-Koehler, 1996.

Wilkinson, L. "How to Build Scenarios." *Wired,* special edition on *Scenarios: The Future of the Future,* 1.01 (1995): 74–81.

WWW Sites of Interest

Analyzing Environments and Developing Scenarios for Uncertain Times
http://sunsite.unc.edu/horizon/welcome/JBChapter.html

> Here you will find James L. Morrison and Ian Wilson's chapter from *Planning and Management for a Changing Environment: A Handbook on Redesigning Postsecondary Institutions* edited by Marvin Peterson, David Dill, and Lisa Mets and published by Jossey-Bass.

Boston Chapter of the World Futures Society
www.lucifer.com/~sasha/refs/wfsgbc.html

> At this home site of the World Futures Society there are good links to many "futuring" groups.

Futureweb
www.cl.uh.edu/futureweb/

> This website has excellent links to futures resources. It is the website of the studies of the future program at the University of Houston–Clear Lake.

Global Business Network, P. Schwartz
www.gbn.org

> This site is home to the author of *The Art of the Long View*. It contains lots of information on scenarios and examples.

SRI Consulting
www.sri.com/sric/technology-management/scenarios.html
> The site outlines the SRI approach to scenario planning.

Strategic Futures International
www.sfutures.com
> The site contains information on strategic forecasting and strategic management.

Index

Note: Page numbers for figures are in italic type.

Abstract thinking, 6
Academic libraries, 95
Advocacy skills versus inquiry skills, 40
"Alice's Restaurant" (scenario), 72–5
"All American Arlington" (scenario), 66–9
Allgeier, Marsha, 47
Arabs, viii
Arlington County Public Libraries, ix, 47–78
  achievements and lessons learned, 62–6
  demographics of, 47–8
  Factor Ranking, 53–5
  library planning team (LPT), 49–52
  Matrix of Most-Important Elements, 56
  Scenario Matrix, 58
  scenario planning process, 52–60
  scenario stories, 66–78
  strategic directions, 49, 60–1, 65
  vision and mission statements, 61–2, 65
Art of the Long View, The (Schwartz), 10, 29, 53, 81
Assumptions, 39–41
  hidden, 27
Automation, 102–3
Autonomy versus collaboration, 101–2

Barker, Joel, *Discovering the Future*, 52
Benton Foundation, 96, 104

Index

"Big gains/big pains" strategies, 22
"Boot Straps" (scenario), 108–9
Brainstorming, 56–7, 82–3, 96
Broadcasting versus narrowcasting, 103
Bryan, Alice, *The Public Librarian*, 97
Busch, Nancy, x, 95–113
Bushing, Mary, 100–1

Carbo, Toni, 97–8
Caulfield, Brian, 104
Central point or decision in scenario development, 8–10
Challenge and response scenario plot, 14, 19–30
Change
  in environment, 19, 90
  frequency and unpredictability of, 19
  monitoring in scenarios, 15–16
  in public library field, 95
  resistance to, 27–8
  writing for, 27–32
Child-care services, 88–9
Cincotta, Andy, 47–78
City councils, 96
Cline, Elizabeth, 47
Collaborations with other agencies, 105
Common knowledge, 11
Communitarian ideals, 56
Community instability, 47
Community networking, 102
Community renewal versus decline, 101–2
Competition for students, 11
Concrete thinking, 6
Confidentiality, 51
Consensus, 9, 16, 51
Consistency, internal, 15
Contingent strategies, 22–5
Continuous learning, 34–5, 63

  See also Education;
    Organizational learning
Continuous training, 61
  See also Training
Control and planning, 47
Conventional wisdom, 15
Costs, 11
County manager form of government, 48
Creative thinking, 34, 42
Crisis management versus planning, vii, 19
Culture, 14
Curriculum reform, 98
Customer service, 48, 61, 63, 79, 90
Cycles scenario plot, 14, 31

Data gathering, 37
Decision making, 14, 15
Demographic trends, 4, 12, 30
Discovering the Future (Barker), 52
Discussion, 9
Distance education, 101
Diversity, 48
Diversity of planning groups for scenarios, 10
Donnellan, Barbara, 47
Driving forces, 4, 8
  in Nebraska public libraries, 97–101
  in scenario planning, 11–12
  in UNL student technology fee scenario planning, 82–3

Economic information (in STEEP), 8
Education
  distance, 101
  information on, 8, 11
  and the Internet, 103–4
  national and multistate cooperation in, 101

of Nebraska public librarians, 95–113
See also Continuous learning; Organizational learning; Training
Edwards, Greg, 52
Eight scenario development steps, 8–16
Electronic newspapers, 103
Emal, Jim, 79–94
Emporia (Kansas) State University School of Library and Information Management Distance Program, 99
Empowerment of staff, 48, 63
Environment, changing, 19, 90
Environmental forces and trends in scenarios, 10–11
Environmental information (in STEEP), 8
Equality of opportunity, 56
Ethical use of information, 97, 98
Evaluation of scenario process, 60
Evolution scenario plot, 14, 30
Exactness versus "fuzziness," 6
Experimentation, 36, 42
External conditions, 27–8
Extrapolation, *4*
  linear, 19

Factor Ranking in Arlington County Public Libraries, 53–5
Filters, information, 28
Fisher, Carl, 47
Fixed strategies, 23
Flexibility, 10, 24, 37, 52, 90, 111
"Fly in the hierarchy" rule, 64
Focus groups, 97
Focus of concern in scenarios, 8
Forecasting future, 7
Four Possible Scenarios for a Pharmaceutical Company, *21*
Friedman, Ann, 47–78

Funding, 61
  competition for, 104–5
  See also Resources
Future
  and organizational learning, 43
  predicting or forecasting, 7, 52
  reasons for planning for, 47–78
  study of, 3–4
  techniques to study, *4*
Futures
  plausible, 20, 23
  possible, 5
  preferable, 5
  probable, 4–5
  types of, 4–5
Futuring Matrix, *4*
"Fuzziness" versus exactness, 6, 16

Garvin, David, 36–7, 42
Gershfeld, Carolyn, 47
Giesecke, Joan, ix, 18–25, 26–33, 34–43, 79–94
Goldberg, Lisbeth, 47
Government policy, changes in, 19
Graduate schools of library and information science, 98, 99, 101, 104, 112
Group processes, 9, 38–9, 42

Hayes, Ellen, 47
Hidden assumptions, 27
"High Technology Skill" (scenario), 91–2
High-performance organization (HPO), 48, 49
Hornick, Scot, 18–25
Horton, Betty, 47
HPO. *See* High-performance organization

Immigrant population, 48, 62
"Impending Obscurity" (scenario), 105–7

Index

Implications of scenarios, 15, 20, 22
"In the box" thinking, 40
Indicators for monitoring change in scenarios, 15–16
Infinite possibilities scenario plot, 14, 31
Information age, 98
Information field, 20, 98
Information filters, 28
Information for scenarios (STEEP), 8
Information service (IS), 80, 89
Information services personalization, 103–4
Information technology proliferation, 102–3
Institute of Alternative Futures, 53
Internal consistency, 15
Internal inertia, 27
Internet, 30–1, 101, 102, 103
Intuitive thinking, 6
IS. *See* Information service

King, James, ix, 3–17
Knowledge
  common, 11
  transferring, 36, 42

LAMA. *See* Library Administration and Management Association
LAMA/LITA National Conference program on scenario planning, x
"Last Hope" (scenario), 107–8
Laws of probability, 20
Leadership, 51, 63
Learning organizations. *See* Organizational learning
Learning. *See* Continuous learning; Education; Organizational learning

"Let Them Eat Cake" (scenario), 75–8
Lewally, Kadija, 47
Libraries for the Twenty-First Century, 96
Library Administration and Management Association (LAMA), x
Library and information science graduate schools, 98, 99, 101, 104, 112
Library and Information Technology Association (LITA), x
Library boards, 48, 96, 100
Library Journal, 97
Library management, vii–viii
Limited resources, 47
Linear extrapolation, 19
LITA. *See* Library and Information Technology Association
Lone Ranger scenario plot, 14, 31
Losing strategies, 22
"Low Technology Skill" (scenario), 92–4
Lund, Anne, 47

McQuade, Jayne, 47
Management groups, 58–9
Management of libraries, vii–viii
Managing the Portfolio of Strategic Options, 25
Master's Degree in Library and Information Science, 99
Matrix of Most-Important Elements in Arlington County Public Libraries, 56
Matrix of Uses of Technology to Enhance Student Learning at UNL, 83
Mediacy skills, 97–8, 104
Medical Library Association, 98
Mental models, viii, 6, 27, 90

Mercer, David, 81, 82
Middle class, 56
Millennium fever, 97
Mini-scenarios, 82
Mission statements, ix, 61–2, 65
My generation scenario plot, 14, 32

Narrative sequence in scenarios, 13–15, 22, 32–3
Narrative structuring, 8
Nebraska Library Association, 111
Nebraska Library Commission, 95, 99, 110–11
Nebraska public libraries, x, 95–113
   certification program for librarians, 100–1
   collaborations with other agencies, 105
   dimensions of uncertainty in, 101–2
   driving forces, 97–101
   funding competition, 104–5
   implications and strategies from scenarios, 110–12
   information service personalization, 103–4
   information technology proliferation, 102–3
   key stakeholders, 95–6, 111
   librarians in, 99–100
   Scenario Matrix, *102*
   Scenario Matrix for Libraries of the Future, *105*
   scenario stories, 105–10
   sources of input for scenario building, 96–7
   statistics on, 99
"New Horizons" (scenario), 109–10
"Niche news," 103
"No-brainer" strategies, 22
"No-painer" strategies, 22

Ogilvy, Jay, 51, 53
Oil crisis, viii
Olson, Robert, 53, 59
Options on strategies, 23–4
Organizational learning, ix, 6, 15, 34–7
   definition of, 26
   disciplines for
      building a shared vision, 35, 41
      group learning, 35, 38–9
      mental models, 35, 39–41
      personal mastery, 35, 37–8
      systems thinking, 35, 41–2
   for the future, 43
   management strategies for, 36–7, 42
   measurement of, 37
   and scenario planning, 37–42
   See also Continuous learning; Education
Organizations
   resistance to change in, 27–8
   values and visions in, 26
"Out of the box" thinking, 6, 42, 52

Palmer School of Library and Information Science, 97
Personalization of information services, 103–4
Planning, 4
   and control, 47
   process of, vii–x
   and scenarios, 26
   techniques of, vii, 20, 27
   versus crisis management, 19
   vision and mission statement in, 61–2
Plausible futures, 20, 23
Plots of scenarios, 14, 29–32
Political information (in STEEP), 8
Possible futures, 5

126 Index

Possible Uses for the UNL Technology Fee, 87
Prediction of future, 7, 20, 22
Preferable futures, 5
Probability laws, 20
Probable futures, 4–5
Professional development of librarians, 95–113
Program quality, 11
Property taxes, 104
"Proposition 13" (scenario), 69–72
Public forums, 96
Public Librarian, The (Bryan), 97
Public librarian certification program in Nebraska, 100–1
Public library and information practitioners in Nebraska. *See* Nebraska public libraries
Public opinion surveys, 96–7
Public policy and access issues, 102–3

Qualitative measures, 37
Qualters, Roger, 47–78
Quantitative measures, 37
Question (focus of concern) in scenarios, 8
Quinn, Brian, 66

Ranking forces in scenarios, 12
Ranking methods, 12
Real-world actions, 16
Regional library systems, 95
Research, 12, 50, 52–3, 96
Resources, limited, 47
   See also Funding
Revolution scenario plot, 14, 30–1
Road map paradigm, 18, 19–20
Robinson, Cathy, 47–78
Robust strategies, 22–5
Royal Dutch Shell Corporation, viii
Rural public libraries and librarians, 99–101

Sales taxes, 104
SAST (strategic assumption surfacing and testing), 27
Scanning techniques, 12, 16
Scenario matrices
   of Arlington County Public Libraries, 56, 58
   for Nebraska public libraries, 102, 105
   for a pharmaceutical company, 21
   for UNL Student Technology Fee, 83, 86
Scenarios, viii–x, 5–16
   of Arlington County Public Libraries, 66–78
   criteria for development of, 14–15, 26–7
   definition of, viii, 6–8, 20, 32
   diversity of planning groups, 10
   focus of concern in, 8
   LAMA/LITA National Conference program on, x
   mini, 82
   naming of, 32–3
   for organizational learning, 37–42
   outcomes of, 16
   plot lines in, 14, 29–32
   for public libraries, 105–10
   steps in developing, 8–16
   strategies in, 22–5
   structure of, 20–2
   for UNL student technology fee, 91–4
   visioning process for, 20–2
   writing plots, 26–33
      for change, 27–32
      framing the problem, 27
      writing the script, 32–3
School libraries, 95

Index

Schwartz, Peter
  The Art of the Long View, 10, 29, 53, 81
  "Using Scenarios to Navigate the Future," 34
Seasonal trends, 10
Senge, Peter, 35, 37–42
Shopping on the Internet, 103
Snyder, David, 52
Social information (in STEEP), 8
Social structure of society, changes in, 19
Special libraries, 95
Special Libraries Association, 98
Staff
  communications with, 57–9
  competencies of, 11
  and continuous learning, 35, 63
  education and training of, 95–113
  empowerment of, 48, 63
  involvement with scenario process, 59–60
Stargazer Gazette, The (newsletter), 57
STEEP (social, technological, economic, environmental, and political issues), 8, 10–11, 12
Steps in developing scenarios
  central point or decision, 8–10
  driving forces, 4, 8, 11–12, 82–3
  environmental forces and trends, 10–11
  implications, 15
  indicators for monitoring change, 15–16
  main themes, 13
  narrative sequence, 13–15, 32–3
  ranking the forces, 12
Strategic assumption surfacing and testing (SAST), 27
Strategic directions, 49, 60–3, 65
Strategic planning techniques. *See* Planning, techniques of
Strategic-trend intelligence, 12

Structuring the narrative, 8
Students
  competition for, 11
  on scenario teams, 81
  support of, 88–9
  See also UNL student technology fee
Surprises, 18, 19
SWOT (strengths, weaknesses, opportunities, and threats) analysis, 15

Taxes, 104
Team members, 9, 39, 64
Teamwork, 48, 50–1, 53
Technological information (in STEEP), 8
Technology, 61
  changes in, 19, 47, 63, 97
  and public libraries, 103
Telecommuting, 102
Themes or assumptions in scenarios, 13
Thinking
  concrete, abstract, and intuitive, 6
  creative, 34, 42
  "in the box," 40
  "out of the box," 6, 42, 52
  types of, 4
Total quality management (TQM), vii, 36
Training
  continuous, 61
  "train-the-trainer" approach, 63
  See also Education
Transferring knowledge, 36, 42
Tunnel vision, 19

University of Michigan School of Information, 98
University of Nebraska–Lincoln. *See* UNL student technology fee

University of Pittsburgh School of Information Sciences, 97
UNL student technology fee, ix, 79–94
  action steps, 89
  assessment, 89–90
  background, 80–1
  drivers for change, 82–3
  identifying issues, 85–7
  key factors, 83–4
  Matrix of Uses of Technology, *83*
  Possible Uses for, *87*
  research and benefit assessment, 88
  Scenario Matrix, *86*
  scenario stories for, 91–4
  student support of, 88–9
"Using Scenarios to Navigate the Future" (Schwartz), 34

Values, 14, 41
  organizational, 26
Virtual workplaces, 102
Vision
  organizational, 26
  shared, 41
Vision statements, ix, 61–2, 65
Vision 2020, 52
Visioning process, 20–2
Visioning sessions, 96

Wack, Pierce, viii
Winners and losers scenario plot, 14, 29
Wired (magazine), 104
Wisdom, conventional, 15
Woodsworth, Anne, 97
Workplaces, virtual, 102
World Wide Web, 30–1, 81, 88, 119–20

Joan Giesecke is the Dean of Libraries, University of Nebraska–Lincoln Libraries. She has received a doctorate in public administration from George Mason University, an MLS from the University of Maryland, a master's degree in management from Central Michigan University, and a BA in economics from SUNY at Buffalo. Giesecke's research interests include organizational decision making and management skills. She has developed a training program for managers and has presented a variety of papers on management and supervisory skills. She is a former editor of *Library Administration and Management* and has published numerous articles on management issues.